Cryptids of The World

A conclusive guidebook to the menagerie of enigmatic animals seen across our natural world

By Ryan Edwards

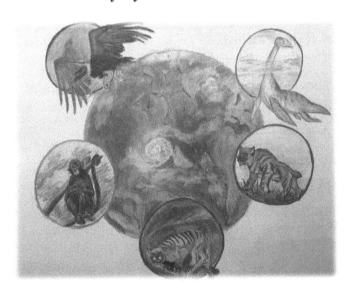

Ryan Edwards

Introduction

What are cryptids? A cryptid is an animal whose existence is not yet proven by science. The particular science dedicated to the study of these enigmatic creatures is called cryptozoology. The individuals who study these creatures are called cryptozoologists; their job is to try to discover these creatures using proven scientific methods. Some of the most well-known cryptids are bigfoot, Nessie and the yeti. Even with these more well-known cryptids there are many others like the agogwe, ninki-nanka, the Beast of Bray Road, and many more. Many mainstream scientists take cryptozoology as a pseudoscience or as just a fun hobby. This misconstrued ideology can be made by a simple lack of knowledge on this field. At first glance cryptozoology might have the appearance of just a few misguided individuals going on a wild goose chase for monsters, but there is more to this. There are academic minds and scientific thinking in this field that hopefully bring more validation to the study of unknown species. Yes, there will always be skepticism in this field, but one must not let a skeptical view become one of ridicule. Even individuals within cryptozoology should use skeptical thinking in their research. A healthy skepticism should be welcomed in this community not seen as hindrance. A cryptozoologist must come to a logical scientific conclusion using empirical, not just anecdotal evidence; even though that is a cryptozoologist's bread and butter. So, one must walk a tightrope of skepticism and optimism or scientific fact and belief. A belief in these creatures is always warranted but this can sometimes cause one to go down a path divergent from science and logic. The scientific method is about knowing something exists, not just believing it does. In this book you will face some astounding theories and some extreme conclusions that are mostly formed primarily from scientific ideals. Even though these theories and conclusions are my own, it doesn't mean they are truly factual. You might even form your own conclusions after reading this book that are polar opposites of my own. The field of cryptozoology attracts so many characters with their own paradigms and hypotheses. Just because one theory is different from another doesn't mean it should be met with ridicule. Science is about looking at all the data and making conclusions from there. Only through analysis of all the data and evidence can we get to the truth of these animals even if it's a scary one. One thing that can be a damper on cryptozoology is fear. The fear of ridicule, fear of disbelief and most of all the fear of the unknown. Don't be afraid of the unknown, embrace the unknown cause that is when discoveries are made. After you read this book, you will feel different to the natural world due to the fact that you never know what is hiding out there. Humans have sometimes lost a sense of exploration and of discovery. The natural world is divided between "seen" (in a sense of that we already know what's there) and "other." What if we don't know everything to know about our natural world? There are still discoveries to be made and animals not yet recognized. Don't ever think we know everything because we don't. It is only through exploration and inquisitiveness will we find out what truly lives in the farthest reaches of our natural world. Always keep questioning what's out there, always stay inquisitive. Most of all never stop exploring.

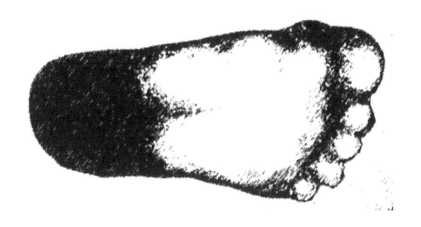

Ryan Edwards

Contents

Ryan Edwards

.

Adjule

The adjule is a canine cryptid seen in the Sahara Desert of Africa. The adjule is distinctively different from other indigenous canine species in the region. The markings of this creature are very different from the local foxes and jackals. The description of the adjule is of a canine with rounded ears, patches of black, yellow, and white fur, with a long bushy tail. Some legends from local peoples state that the adjule only has three toes, but that is not definitive. The Tuareg people use the word "Tarhsit" for the females of the species while the name adjule for the males of the species; but this might not be evidence for the animal being sexually dimorphic. The indigenous people of the region say that the adjule live in packs, similar to most species of canines. Due to the description of the adjule, many researchers think that the adjule is an isolated population of African Wild Dogs. This is because the African Wild Dog has a very similar coat coloring as the adjule. The usual range of the African Wild Dog is Sub-Saharan Africa, but many have suspected that a small population of these endangered canines could have survived in Northern Africa. So due to this some researchers believe that the adjule is a hope for this endangered canine living in an environment in which it was originally not thought to exist.

Agogwe

The agogwe is a mysterious hominid that is seen in the deserted region of East Africa. The agogwe is similar to other unknown primates of Africa and around the world. The bulk of sightings occur on the Ivory coast of Africa. The description of the agogwe is a four-foot-tall primate with wooly rust colored fur and some even say it has a human-like face that has yellow coloration. The distinguishing factor is that the agogwe is seen being biped *(the ability to walk erect on two legs)*, meaning that it could not be a monkey, suggesting a more hominid-like creature. The natives of Africa told legends of the "little people" and soon colonists from Britain heard and saw these "little people" themselves. At first white settlers thought that the agogwe was just a tribe of little people like the pygmies until a closer look they could see the agogwe had a more basal appearance. Many anthropologists have thought that the agogwe were a misidentification of indigenous baboons and chimps, but many have disproved that due to neither one of these species having the ability for prolonged bipedal locomotion. Due to this some have put forward the theory that the agogwe is a relict population of extinct hominid. The cryptozoologist Bernard Heuvelmans did put forward the idea that the agogwe is an *australopithecus*, a hominid that lived in Africa about 4 million years ago. Early *australopithecines* had the appearance of bipedal chimps and are our distant ancestors.

Ahool

The ahool is a flying cryptid seen in the jungles of Java. Most witnesses state that the ahool is most akin to a bat, but one of gigantic proportions. The description of the ahool is of a bat with a 10-foot wingspan, about the size of a human child, black leathery wings, black fur and the most peculiar aspect a monkey-like face. The name for the ahool comes from the vocalization it is said to make; the witnesses of the ahool state it makes a noise like "ahhooool" when it flies. The ahool is supposed to live in caves in the Sakel Mountain range and due to it being nocturnal like most bats it leaves during the night and catches fish and other prey items with its razor-sharp claws. To some people the action of the ahool hunting fish might seem peculiar but this behavior is supported by extant known species of bats. The Mexican fishing bat is a bat species that specializes in hunting fish. It is likely the ahool has gone down a similar dietary path due its great size. The ahool diet can't consist of insects and fruit like other bats due to its large size. Based on descriptions of the ahool most researchers believe it's a yet to be discovered species of giant bat. Others suspect that the ahool is a species of flying primate. This hypothesis is unlikely as there aren't any known mammals capable of flight other than bats. The flying primate theory is created thanks to the supposed simian-like face of the ahool. This description might be due to eyewitnesses misidentifying a bat face and giving it primate-like qualities.

Almasty

Also known as the almas, this cryptid is considered Russia's bigfoot. The almasty has many similarities to bigfoot but also has many differences. The description of the almasty is from 5 to 7 feet tall, human-like, muscular, a heavy brow ridge, and either covered in black to brown fur or wearing animal furs. The major difference between the almas and other unknown primates is that they have a very human-like appearance and behaviors. The almas is said to have a very basic language and culture. Due to this many almasty researchers such as Boris Porshnev think that the almasty is a surviving population of Neanderthals or Denisovans; two supposedly extinct human relatives. The name almasty originated in Mongolia but the sightings of this animal are from Russia's Caucasus Mountains to Siberia.

One of the most famous incidents in almasty history is Zana. The story goes that in the 1850s a "wild woman" was caught by a local landowner as a prize and was even able to have several children. Later DNA testing showed that Zana had Sub-Saharan African DNA, which proves that Zana wasn't some relict Neanderthal. Even though Zana was proven not to be an ancient hominid it doesn't mean the almasty as a whole isn't one. It is possible that due to their high intellect and natural human adaptability, the Neanderthals were able to survive into the modern day, by living in areas that regular people wouldn't be able to reach.

Altamaha-ha

This is an aquatic cryptid that is seen in Georgia's Altamaha River. The creature is mostly seen where the river meets the Atlantic Ocean, this has caused many to think this creature could be a marine animal. The description of the altamaha-ha is of an aquatic creature about 18 feet long, grey to black in color, alligator-like snout, smooth skin like an eel, a long body with a long tail, two forward flippers and a long neck. The witnesses state that when they see the altamaha-ha it moves its tail up and down causing many to theorize that this creature could be a new species of marine mammal. The first sightings of the altamaha-ha occurred in 1969. The witnesses would usually see the creature's long neck and head sticking out of the water similar to Scotland's Nessie. Witnesses would see a line of humps in the water as if they were a part of a larger animal. There were also splashes in the water too large to be caused by any indigenous animals. Most investigators and cryptozoologists believe that the altamaha-ha is a new species of marine animal which has made its home in the Altamaha River based on the movement of the tail and that some witnesses describe a blowhole being present on the animal. If this creature is presumed to be a new species of marine mammal, is it likely it is a new species of pinniped. It is also possible that these sightings might be caused by a known species of pinniped that has found itself in the brackish water of the Altamaha River.

Alux

The alux is a diminutive unknown primate seen in Central America. Folklore of the alux originates from the native Mayan people of the Yucatan Peninsula. According to the Mayans the alux is a race of small primitive people that live in the jungles. Stories regarding alux are similar to the stories of European fairies and leprechauns. The usual description of the alux is of a human-like bipedal primate, standing around 3 to 5 feet tall, covered in black to red hair and possesses primitive human-like facial features. The alux are seen as being intelligent, living in family groups and might even use basic tools. The Maya believed the alux could be helpful if treated nicely or destructive if treated with disrespect. There are similar belief systems in several cultures around the world which speak of forest people or even small human-like beings which live in the wilderness. This demonstrates that stories of small human-like beings living in the forest are a global phenomenon. Most people know of fairies, leprechauns, and elves but there exists a myriad of other oral traditions of small humanoid beings who stay on the fringes of human society. Much is just folklore, but others might be proven to be based as a biological species. Since there aren't any indigenous apes in the New World, it is possible that the alux is a whole new form of highly intelligent simian. Stories of the alux might even originate from legends of a primitive race of pygmy-like humans who lived in Central America in the past but have died out in modern times.

Andean Wolf

This is another cryptic canid seen in the world. This particular canid is seen in South America, especially in the Andes Mountains, as the name suggests. The two main regions where this animal has been seen is in eastern Brazil and Argentina. The description of the Andean wolf is of a canine with abnormally long legs, short orange fur on its body, black fur on legs and neck, and rounded ears. From that description many have suspected that the Andean wolf is a population of maned wolf native to Brazil. German animal collector Lorenz Hagenbeck bought three peculiar pelts, thought to be from this creature in Brazil in 1927, and showed them to Germain mammologist Dr. Ingo Krumbiegel, who declared it a new species. Later Hagenbeck brought a skull believed to be from one of these creatures and Dr. Krumbiegel came to the same conclusion; that it is a new species and not a known extant canine. Although Dr. Krumbiegel came to this conclusion, and many agreed with him that the Andean wolf is an entirely new species of canine living in the mountains of the Andes and tropical jungle, most other zoologists believe that it was a regular maned wolf, either misidentified, or just possibly a new subspecies of maned wolf.

Artrellia

The artrellia is an unknown reptilian creature seen in the South Pacific. on the island of Papua New Guinea, where people have been telling tales of this animal for generations. The artrellia is believed to be is a giant arboreal lizard which many consider as a dragon. Settlers started seeing the artrellia in the late 19th century and repeating legends of tree dragons which they saw in the jungle, but the indigenous people have been telling such stories for centuries. The description of the artrellia is of a lizard from 20 to 40 feet long, from grey to green scaled skin, somewhat akin to a giant gecko, from the description. Some of the most credible sightings occurred in the 1940s when GIs went to Papua New Guinea and saw this gigantic creature. In 1980, two researchers tried to find the artrellia in the jungles of New Guinea, with an expedition called "Operation Drake." They did not find an artrellia but they did discovered the Sarvadori's mountain lizard, which many researchers think is the reason for the legend of the artrellia. Aside from that find, there are others with their own theories. Some have developed the idea that the artrellia is a relic population of giant lizards. which lived throughout the South Pacific during the Pleistocene, then went extinct later. It is possible one of these species adapted to become arboreal. Another possibility is that the artrellia is a species of giant gecko.

Atlas Bear

Though it isn't common knowledge, there have been indigenous species of bears on the African continent. The most well-known of these *ursidae* is the Atlas bear of Northern Africa. The Atlas bear is a subspecies of the Old-World brown bear, found in the Atlas Mountains of Morocco and Libya. The description of the Atlas bear is of a bear with a brown coat, 9 feet long about 1000 pounds, 4-inch-long fur and a muzzle shorter than the American grizzly. The Atlas bear flourished until human over-hunting and decline of habitat constricted the Atlas bear to only Morocco. From that point many zoologists believe that the Atlas bear went extinct, never to be seen again. Or was it? Years later many individuals have seen a creature that they describe to have the appearance of the "extinct" Atlas bear. Because of this, many cryptozoologists have concluded that the Atlas bear could have survived the extinction event of the 1870s. If they did, this would make the Atlas bear one of many species believed to still exist, although mainstream scientists believe they are extinct. The name for these species is *Lazarus taxon* with the Atlas bear possibly being one of these. So, does the Atlas bear may still exist in the remote regions of the Atlas Mountains today? We don't know: hopefully if they are, we can rediscover these animals before they meet the fate that most believe this species to have originally.

Baramanu

In the early 1900s when French explorers started going into the Middle East, they heard legends from the many nomadic cultures from the region. One of these legends is of the baramanu which people described as a wild man living in the mountains of the Shishi Valley of Northern Pakistan, where most of the sightings have occurred. Some explorers even heard peculiar howls and vocalizations while in the area which were attributed to the baramanu. The baramanu is described as a human-like bipedal being, 6 to 8 feet tall, with red to black fur which covers the body, and long arms. Many see similarities between the baramanu and North America's bigfoot due to the similar description of the creatures. The indigenous cultures think the baramanu as a part-human beast creature that still roams the mountains of Pakistan. Their stories state that the baramanu is peaceful but when any humans encroach on their territory there is likelihood of a more violent encounter with the baramanu. Many researchers think that the baramanu could be related to two other famous cryptids seen nearby the yeti of the Himalayas and the almas that is seen in Russia and Mongolia. Due to this correlation many researchers think that the baramanu could be a surviving population of Neaderthals just like the almas. Another possibility is that the baramaun could be surviving groups of Denisovans, another human species that lived alongside modern humans and Neanderthals.

Batutut

The batutut is supposedly a small unknown primate seen in the jungles of Southeast Asia, primarily in Malaysia and Vietnam. The one difference that the batutut has than other indigenous primates is that the batutut is human-like and bipedal. The zoologist Dr. John Mackinnon was one of the first western scientists to study the batutut in the 1970s, where he found tracks believed to have been made by this animal. Mackinnon even wrote a book about the batutut, *In Search of The Red Ape*. The description of the batutut is of a hominid-like primate 4 to 6 feet tall, red fur and a very human-like face. Legends of the batutut have survived for generations in Southeast Asia. This has caused many researchers assume that the batutut as a legend, not based in reality. However, a strong oral history can show how the natives know this creature exists in the jungle. Many researchers think that the batutut might be related to other unknown hominids of the region, such as the nguoi-rung spotted in Vietnam and the Bukit Timah monkey man. Some have suspected that all these animals could be the same creature due to the similarities in their description. Many cryptozoologists think the batutut is a relict population of *homo-erectus*, an extinct hominid that's fossils have been found in the same region. *Homo-erectus* was estimated to be about 5 feet tall and believed to be fur covered similar to descriptions of the batutut.

Bear Lake Monster

The Bear Lake Monster is a large aquatic cryptid seen in Bear Lake, situated on the border of the states of Idaho and Utah. The lake is about 20 miles long and about 8 miles wide. Possibly this might be large enough to hide the creature that has been told to live in it. The legend began with native tribes telling tales of a giant "snake" that resided in the lake and could even crawl on score on small legs. Later, when colonists started to come into the area, they saw this creature for themselves. They described the creature as a 20-to-50-foot animal with an elongated body, smooth black to grey skin, and small flippers. In 1871 one of the most famous incidents with this creature occurred: locals reported shooting at a creature that swam like a serpent in the lake. Another individual claimed that they captured a 20-foot-long creature from the lake. Later reports showed that the later incident was simply a hoax. Because of this, many believe that the monster is a myth. For a long time, people considered the creature as merely a local legend, until frequent sightings between 1937 and 1996. Because of those later sightings, many think of the monster as more than a legend. Many researchers think the Bear Lake monster could be an unknown species of giant aquatic snake or giant eel. If the creature is real, sightings have been few and far between in recent decades.

Beast of Bladenboro

This cryptid was first sighted in the town of Bladenboro, North Carolina. The first sightings occurred in 1954 when residents' pets and livestock were going missing, and later being found dead. The manner of death was curious, as they all had been killed in the same way; two puncture holes in the neck and no blood at the scene. After a month the rampage and sightings ended abruptly. Witness described the creature as a cat-like creature about 6 feet long, with a bulky body, short legs, feline-like head, long ears, and short brown fur. Many considered the beast to be vampiric in origin, as there was no blood at the scene. After 1955 the creature was never seen again; leaving most to assume that the creature behind the attacks had left the area. Then, in 2007 there were similar attacks in Bolivia, North Carolina. The details of the killings in Bolivia were similar to the attacks in Bladenboro, fifty years previously. This caused many to believe that the creature had returned, and no one was safe: the residents of North Carolina's pets were being killed in a strange way with no blood and the meat not eaten. Thanks to photographic evidence it was proven that the perpetrator of these attacks was a cougar. Cougars were once found along the East Coast but presumed extinct there in the 1930s. In recent times the cougar has been making a comeback in this region, which might explain the strange series of killings in this part of the country including the ones in Bladenboro during the 1950s.

Ryan Edwards

Beast of Bodmin Moor

The Beast of Bodmin Moor is one of England's most famous cryptids. This feline creature was first seen in Cornwall's Bodmin Moor in the 1990s. The reports usually began with a farmer's livestock being killed and residents seeing a peculiar creature. The description of the animal is of a cat about the size of a cougar, jet black, a long and curved tail, rounded ears, and short fur. But other sightings described the creature as tawny-colored like a cougar. This creature is just one of a long line of cryptid felines in England, such as the Surrey Puma and Beast of Exmoor. Many think that sightings of these animals began in the 1970s when it was fashionable in England to have a big cat as a pet, until when the government outlawed the ownership of exotic animals in 1976. Because of that law, many owners surrendered their animals to local zoos and sanctuaries, while others admitted that they released their animals into the moors to avoid paying a fine. Many have speculated that these released big cats could have created a breeding population in the moors that were able to hide from the eyes of people. Many researchers of these creatures think that it is possible for a breeding population of big cats to survive in the countryside of England. This only leaves us with one question. Is it possible for a sustainable population of big cats to exist in Great Britain, given a lack of suitable habitat, and lack of genetic variation because of the lower number of individual animals?

Beast of Bray Road

The Beast of Bray Road could be one of the scariest cryptids in North America. This canine cryptid is seen primarily on Bray Road outside Elkhorn, Wisconsin. Witnesses described this cryptid as a modern-day werewolf; a canine with short brown to black fur, tall, pointed ears, wolf-like head, bushy tail … and most frequently walking bipedally on two legs. There also have been sightings of the creature walking on all fours like a regular wolf. Though the creature is called the Beast of Bray Road, it has been seen throughout Wisconsin, Ohio, Michigan, and most of the U.S. Midwest. The sightings began in the 1980s when individuals saw a peculiar creature cross Bray Road or in the local woods. Soon a journalist named Linda Godfrey started writing about the sightings of this creature. Later Godfrey even wrote a book called *Real Wolfmen: True Encounters in Modern America* where she writes about her research. Why I like to call these creatures "bipedal canines" is because these canines have a tendency of prolonged bipedal locomotion. I believe these creatures are canines which have developed the ability of bipedalism due to their environment or mutation. These bipedal canines might help explain sightings of the beast of Bray Road and other werewolf-like cryptids.

Beast of Busco

This aquatic cryptid was first sighted in 1889 in Churubusco, Indiana. The story of the beast of Busco started when a farmer named Oscar Fulk saw an enormous turtle in the pond on his property outside of Churubusco. Fulk decided to leave the animal alone and didn't mention the enormous reptile to anyone again. Years later the farm was sold to another family, who also decided to leave the creature alone. This ended in 1949, when a new owner of the land, Hale Harris, and several other residents of town saw the creature. The witnesses describe an animal similar to a turtle; a snapping turtle about 12 feet in diameter, with a green shell, short tail and long claws on every foot protruding out of the shell. Soon Harris named the creature "Oscar" after the original witness of the creature. The creature is also known as the "Beast of Busco". People from all over came to try to see and even capture the animal. Harris himself tried to drain the lake but "Oscar" was still not found. This miraculous vanishing act might be explained by the possible existence of caves in the lake that let the animal escape. Even the local Miami tribe told legends of a giant turtle, which lived in the lake; so large they could dock their canoes on it. Could this animal be the same as "Oscar" that is seen today? Most speculate that this animal is a giant alligator snapping turtle which has been able to survive in this lake for decades.

Beast of Exmoor

This is a cryptid feline spotted in England. The sightings began in the 1970s when residents near Exmoor saw a peculiar animal skulking around the area and the depredation on local livestock by an unknown predator. Witnesses described the animal as a big cat with short jet-black fur, a curved long tail, rounded ears and yellow eyes. The livestock killed were primarily sheep. When big cat experts analyzed the fatal wounds, it was evident that they were inflicted by a feline; bitten at the jugular vein while canines usually bite at the hindquarters. Mass hysteria soon spread in the surrounding area, because of the presence of the beast and the inherent danger it possessed. The fear was so strong that the British government sent the Royal Marines to the area of Exmoor to hunt for the beast and to try to kill it if needed. The Marines did not find the beast even though there were some Marines who stated they saw an animal which matched the description of the beast while in the field. With a lack of evidence, the marines withdrew, and the attacks kept occurring. The Beast of Exmoor is just one of a menagerie of other cryptid felines spotted in Britain. Surrey Puma sightings began occurring in the 1960s while the Beast of Bodmin Moor sightings happened later in the 1970s. These felines are most likely the same cats that were released in the 1970s; different names for them have been given according to the location where each particular animal was seen.

Beast of Gevaudan

Possibly one of the most infamous occurrences of a canine cryptid in history is the Beast of Gevaudan. This story started in 1764 when residents of the French province of Gevaudan were being killed by a mysterious predator. The people who survived an attack said that the animal was a *loup-garou* or werewolf. The description of the animal was a canine about 8 feet long, very bulky, with grey fur, long tail, and pointed ears. Many locals suspected that a werewolf made its hunting grounds in the area. The killings were so persistent that the king of France sent his best hunters and soldiers to kill the beast but without success. The soldiers did kill several large wolves in the province. The attacks continued until 1767, when a hunter named Jean Chastel killed the beast with a silver bullet, but that was not the end of the story. The attacks did end but many were still wondering what the creature was. Chastel stated that he lost the body of the creature. It seemed that the mystery was never to be solved until 1997, when a curator in the Paris Museum found a specimen supposed to be the Beast of Gevaudan. The specimen was a spotted hyena, a predator indigenous to Africa. It could be that Chastel used a trained hyena to kill people, in order become famous after killing the creature the end. Ironic, as because the original culprit was suspected to be a werewolf, a mix of man and beast … but in the end, the culprit <u>was</u> a man and a beast.

Bessie

Bessie is a lake monster seen in Lake Erie, the United States. Also known as South Bay Bessie as most sightings occur in the South Bay area of Lake Erie. Sightings for the creature began in 1973 and still occur today. Most witnesses describe the creature in the lake as an aquatic animal about 30 to 40 feet long, very snake-like, with grey-colored skin and around a foot in diameter. Most sighting are reported by boaters on the lake, who see a large shape in the water or humps protruding out of the water. Many think that these can be attributed to boat wakes or misidentifications of known animals in the lake. The belief in this lake monster was so strong that once an individual offered 100,000 dollars for the animal if it was captured. After initial sightings in 1973, they died down in the 1990s, leading many to conclude the animal was dead or even moved to a new area. Later research has revealed a long-time belief of an unknown animal living in the lake. Researchers think that Bessie simply could be a misidentification of known animals or waves made by boats in the lake. Aside from that, others think that Bessie could be a giant eel. Another more probable explanation is that Bessie was just a marketing ploy in order to bring tourists to the lake. With the sightings only starting in the 1970s and ending in the 1990s it is likely this creature wasn't real at all and was just a way to bring publicity to Lake Erie.

Big Bird

The first sightings of this cryptid occurred in the Rio Grande Valley of Texas in the 1970s. Those who witnessed this flying cryptid described the creature as looking like a pterosaur-like animal or a giant bird; a flying animal with leathery wings, either a long beak or no beak, and a small body with a wingspan of about 20 feet wide. The residents of South Texas would see a peculiar animal in the sky, but there were also sightings of a strange creature on the ground. People said that they saw a figure about 6 feet tall with a shape like a large bird. The sightings only lasted about 2 weeks, which caused some to think that this could be an animal on its migratory route, which just happened to be seen. Although this cryptid is named after a beloved cartoon character this creature does not have such a benign temperament. In 1976, a Brownsville, Texas, man named Alverico Guajardo was attacked by a creature. He said was a giant bat, which picked him up and was very violent. Later cryptozoologists have made the theory that big bird could have been a species of extinct pterosaur called a *quetzalcoatlus* of which fossils have only been found in the Rio Grande Valley. I am of the opinion that the big bird was just a cryptid known as a thunderbird and the descriptions of a pterosaur were just misidentification. Another possibility is that the big bird event is an example of a flying humanoid phenomena, primarily seen in northern Mexico.

Bigfoot

One of the most famous cryptids of all time is the one and only bigfoot. The name bigfoot describes a large unknown primate seen in North America which has been told in aboriginal folklore for centuries. The name bigfoot originates in 1956 when the logger Jerry Crew in Northern California discovered huge footprints in the Bluff Creek drainage. Soon Crew showed the prints to the local newspaper which named the creature "Bigfoot" after the huge footprints it left. Years later one of the most controversial videos in cryptozoology was shot by two men named Roger Patterson and Bob Gimlin. It shows a female bigfoot walking along a riverbank in northern California. Most people that analyze this video believe it to be genuine. The usual description of bigfoot is of a bipedal primate about 6 to 9 feet tall, with black to red fur, large feet, pointed head, long arms, prominent brow, barrel chest and a human-like face. Some of the best evidence for bigfoot are footprints that cannot be identified, video clips, and unknown primate-like vocalizations and wood knocks. There are several theories on the origination of Bigfoot. One of the most popular theories states that a giant extinct ape called *gigantopithecus* that lived in China during the Pleistocene epoch. Researchers believe *gigantopithecus* crossed the Bering Strait land bridge that connected Asia to North America. This giant ape might be living to this day; the identification of bigfoot with *gigantopithecus* evolved once it reached North America, which is what bigfoot eyewitnesses see today.

Big Grey Man

Also known as the Big Grey Man of Ben Macdhui, this is a bigfoot-like cryptid seen in Scotland. This creature is seen primarily in and around Ben Macdhui, one of the tallest mountains in the British Isles. The locals think that this creature makes its home on Ben Macdhui where it hides away from people in the thick mist. The individuals that see the grey man describe it as a human-like figure about 6 to 8 feet tall with short grey hair covering the entire body. Others say that they don't even see the creature, they just have a feeling of another presence in the woods with them that wants them to leave, and they do. This feeling does have some similarities to bigfoot sightings in the United States. Due to that some have made the idea that the grey man is not a physical being and is a spirit or metaphysical being residing on Ben Macdhui. Some have seen similarities of the Big Grey Man to the woodwuse of other parts of the United Kingdom, as both are similar to the North America's bigfoot. What the big grey man is supposed to be is a creature similar to other unknown primates seen across the world. The one problem is that Scotland does not and has never had indigenous primates let alone a hominid species. At one time the British Isles were connected to the European mainland via land bridges. It is possible that a hominid species living in Europe like the Neanderthals were able to cross these bridges and are still persist in the remote regions of the U.K.

Bipedal Canines

The Michigan dogman, the Veast of Bray Road, and the rougarou are all instances of Bipedal Canines. Bipedal Canines is the name I use for describing a canine observed to regularly walk on two legs instead of all four. The other most common colloquial name for these creatures is dogman. I refrain from this naming due to the fact that it gives a sense of hybridization of canine and human which is factually erroneous. It is possible that Europe's folklore of werewolves originated from an oral tradition of Bipedal Canines or even individuals seeing these creatures themselves. The origins of these creatures are speculative at best but here's what I suspect. Canids first evolved in North America around 30 million years ago. It is possible that because of environmental changes during the Cenozoic that a genus of canine was able to develop an ability for bipedal locomotion. One problem is that canids are digitigrade, meaning that they walk on their toe pads, are not plantigrade like humans and bears. This can be overcome, as there are instances of dogs who have had their front limbs amputated, or who were born without them, who have learned to walk on their hind feet. This demonstrates that the canine muscular and skeletal structure can support a bipedal existence. This could possibly cause a permanent mutation in a genus of canines which allow them the ability to walk bipedally permanently with intermediate periods of quadrapedic locomotion, permitting them to hide in plain sight.

Black Dogs

This is a term used for cryptid canines that have been seen for centuries, most usually in England and other parts of the British Isles. These are very similar to devil dogs, in that they could have a more astral presence than devil dogs seen across the world. The majority of black dog legends originate in England and Scotland folklore and their mysterious moors. You can even see them in Sir Arthur Conan Doyle's book *Hounds of the Baskervilles* which tells of ghostly black dogs that roam the moors at night. The usual description of black dogs is of a canine larger than a regular domestic dog, short black fur and are often seen with fiery red eyes. Many consider these dogs as an astral presence or a spirit of some sort and not a physical being. Others believe these creatures to be living fresh-and-blood canines which have been able to live undetected in the moors for centuries. Because of the long history of sightings of these creatures, spanning such a vast area, it is hard to judge if these creatures are just simple folktales and legends. It has demonstrated in the past that legends have some root in reality; this just might be another example of that. These animals could be similar to the phenomena of the litany of black panthers and cryptid felines seen in the British Isles. These black dogs, if they are physical beings, might be predators which have hidden in Britain for centuries, and because of their mysterious nature have been altered over time in order to make them more spiritual and ethereal in nature.

Black Panthers

Black panthers are a subset of cryptid feline seen across North America and Europe. All these cryptids are described in the same way, they are felines about the size of a cougar, sleek black fur, rounded ears and a long tail. In the U.S the majority of the sightings of these creatures occur on the East Coast and parts of the Midwest and South. Many cryptozoologists have made the theory that these animals are cats which survived the Pleistocene epoch. They call these creatures *panthera atrox* after the American Lion of the same name which lived in North America. Eyewitnesses describe a large cat larger than a lion with a mane. I'm not fully convinced that the lion sightings in North America are due to the American Lion as the American Lion didn't have a mane. It is possible that the genus *Panthera atrox* has survived into the modern day. Because of the sheer size of this animal, it would have to live in parts of Canada and Alaska, because of the larger prey species in those regions. As for the sightings of black panthers in North America they are most likely escaped exotic cats; black leopards, jaguars, and melanistic cougars. Cougars have been returning to areas that they were forced out of hundreds of years ago. There has been an increase of cougar sightings along the East Coast and there's an increase of black panther sightings too. I believe these are connected, as both of these cats belong to the same species.

Brosnya

Residents of Lake Brosno, Russia, some 250 miles away from Moscow are afraid of a dragon. This is not the type to fly around stealing livestock and riches; this supposedly inhabits their local lake. Reports of a large aquatic beast that lives in the lake have been around for about 150 years, but the local folklore holds that a creature has been living in the lake for centuries. One tale even states that an invading army was killed while along the shore of Lake Brosno in the 13th century by this creature. The description of Brosnya is of an aquatic serpentine animal with a snake-like head, smooth black to grey colored skin and no identifiable fins or flippers. Most of the sightings occur to individuals along the lake when they see a large shape or humps in the water, which is supposed to belong to the dragon. There is anecdotal evidence that states that it is possible that this animal could be semi-aquatic as there are stories that it can come out of the water and eat livestock. Some explanations of this animal is that it could be a misidentification of debris or logs in the lake and which have floated to the surface. Another explanation is that it could be a large sturgeon of a new species of giant eel or fish.

Bukit Timah Monkey Man

The Bukit Timah Monkey Man is another instance of an unknown primate seen in Southeast Asia. This cryptid is seen in Singapore, where it is mostly sighted in the deeply forested regions of Bukit Timah, which gives the creature its' name. The description of the monkey man is of a bipedal human-like primate, 4 to 6 feet tall, with red to black colored fur covering the whole body, and a very primitive-looking human-like face. The indigenous population of the region have told stories of a human-like creature living in the forest, but it wasn't until in the 1800s when colonists came to the region that they started hearing legends of these animals and even saw the animals themselves. The Bukit Timah Monkey Man is also known as BTM or BTMM for short. The BTM has not been really thoroughly researched by Western cryptozoologists due to the remote regions where it supposedly lives, and the overall lack of sightings for this particular cryptid. One of the most famous cryptozoologists who has studied this animal was Karl Shuker. Many have suspected that the BTM is related to other unknown primates in the region like nguoi-rung and the batutut; it is thought that the BTM is a surviving population of hominids like *homo-erectus* or *paranthropus*.

Bunyip

The bunyip is a semi-aquatic cryptid seen in Australia. The bunyip originated in the legends of the Aborigines of Australia who told legends of a creature which inhabited the lakes, rivers and billabongs of the country. Each culture of Australia had their own animal that they identified as a bunyip. The main origin story for the bunyip relates that a person named Bunyip ate a sacred totem animal. For this crime the Rainbow Serpent turned the person into a creature that will forever live in the water. This is only one of many stories of the bunyip. Because of so many stories there is no one singular description for the bunyip. One states it is like an aquatic dog; another is of a serpent with the feathers and beak of a bird and a third describes it as resembling a pinniped. When English settlers came to Australia they heard about the bunyip from the Aborigines and at first didn't believe in it. Then they started seeing the animal themselves. They said it was similar to the bunyip that the Aborigines told them about; a semi-aquatic animal with fur and a large body. There have been very few sightings of the bunyip in modern times, causing many to conclude that they are extinct. Many researchers think that the bunyip could have been an unknown species of pinniped, while others theorize the bunyip could have been a cultural memory of the menagerie of prehistoric megafauna which once dwelled in Australia.

Buru

The buru is an unknown species of lizard seen in central Asia. primarily in the Himalayas and northern India. The buru is believed to be a monitor lizard about 20 feet long which hides in the tropical alpine valleys of the Himalayas. Most sightings of the buru occurred in the 1940s. In 1948 the *London Daily Mail* newspaper sent an expedition in order to discover physical evidence of the buru. The buru was part of local indigenous culture for hundreds of years but it wasn't until the great increase in British exploration in the 1940s that the existence of the buru became known to the western world and cryptozoologists. The description of the buru is of a monitor lizard about 20 feet long, with green scaled skin, and long claws. Some say that it is semi-aquatic and lives in the local swamps and marshes. Soon in the 1950s the sightings of the buru ceased, causing many to suspect that the buru had already gone extinct. The cryptozoologist Bernard Heuvelmans theorized that the buru is an extinct monitor lizard, which reached about double the size as the extant Komodo dragon or even a mainland population of Komodo dragons. He thought that it was possible that the buru could have been the last surviving population of these animals, animals which were supposed to have gone extinct in the Pleistocene era but thanks to human encroachment actually went extinct during the 1950s.

Caddy

Caddy is a cryptid that's reported in the Cadboro Bay in British Columbia, Canada. This creature is also known as cadborosaurus, as it is described as being similar to a dinosaur. The description of the caddy is of a serpentine aquatic creature, about 30 feet long, with two forward flippers that act as propulsion for the creature, a horse-like head, and smooth grey skin. Some eyewitnesses state they see a mane along the back. The residents of Cadboro Bay usually see the creature's back when it protrudes out of the water, on other occasions, individuals only see a horse-like head protruding out of the water. There have been over 200 sightings of Caddy since the 1930s when it was first sighted, although most evidence is anecdotal. In 1937 a carcass supposed to belong to the creature was found, but later analysis showed it was actually a baleen whale. Another piece of evidence was the Kelly Nash video, taken in 2009 when a fisherman captured video of a strange animal in Nushagak Bay. The animal in the video is still unidentified, so this might be a good piece of evidence for the existence of caddy. Researchers suspect that Caddy might primarily live in the open ocean and only migrate to Cadboro Bay during certain parts of the year. Most have suspected that caddy is a form of relict marine reptile or a new form of marine mammal.

Cassie

This is another sea serpent seen off the coast of North America. Cassie is seen in Casco Bay, Maine, which many speculate is where the creature lives. Most sightings of Cassie occurred between 1777 and 1877 in New England, especially in Maine where there were hundreds of sightings. Many make connections of Cassie to other very similar sea serpents and aquatic cryptids from across the world. Cassie is described as an aquatic animal about 50 to 120 feet long, with a horse-like head, serpentine body, very fast, without flippers. Since the early 1900s there have not been any sightings of Cassie, leading many to think that Cassie has either died out or moved to a new area. The skeptics thought that the creature was a misidentification of known animals or even debris in the water which eyewitnesses thought were a sea serpent. The cryptozoologist Loren Coleman put forward the theory that Cassie could not have been mistaken for any indigenous species in the area due to the sheer size of the animal, and characteristics not matching with any known animal in the region. Thanks to the pattern of the sightings, Loren Coleman and other researchers have developed the theory that cassie could have been an animal on a migratory route. Thanks to the similarities between their morphologies, it's possible that Cassie is even the same animal known as Chessie which has been seen in the Chesapeake Bay.

Champ

Sometimes known as America's Loch Ness Monster, this is a lake creature seen in America. Champ is seen in Lake Champlain that is on the border of New York, Vermont, and Canada. The indigenous tribes told legends of a creature which lived in the lake but the first westerner to see the beast was Samuel de Champlain, for whom the lake was named. Champlain described a creature as big around as a barrel living in the lake. When colonists came to the shores of the lake, they also saw a peculiar aquatic creature in the lake. The common description of champ is a creature about 10 to 20 feet long, with a short tail, four flippers, a long neck with a small head resembling a snake's, humps on the creature's body and green to grey skin. From this description many have suspected that Champ could be an extinct marine reptile called a *plesiosaur*, which could have survived in the lake for thousands of years. One of the best pieces of evidence is a photo that supposedly shows Champ, taken by a woman named Sandra Mansi in 1977, showing a creature with a small head on a long neck, connected to a body that was under the water. There have also been instances of echolocation occurring in the lake. Echolocation has only been known to occur in cetaceans and marine mammals. This suggests that Champ is actually a type of dolphin or other aquatic mammal that has found its way into the lake.

Chessie

Chessie is the name for a local sea serpent seen in the Chesapeake Bay of Maryland. Sightings of this cryptid date back to the 19th century. In 1840 a man and two others reported seeing a strange creature in the water, near North Point Maryland, a creature which resembled a giant snake. In 1982 a man named Robert Frew took a video near Kent Island which is believed to depict Chessie. The video depicts a long serpentine-like animal swimming in the water. A panel of the video was sent to the Smithsonian Institute in 1982 to try to identify the animal in the video but their findings were inconclusive. The description of Chessie is of a serpentine creature that is about 12 to 30 feet long with smooth grey skin and no discernible fins or flippers. The sightings were so believed that in 1985 a movement to encourage the scientific study of Chessie; This was stopped due to a "lack of definitive evidence" and funding. Even today there are sightings of Chessie, with one of the most recent occurring in 2014 when an individual stated that they saw a creature similar to a giant eel in the bay. Some of the hypotheses put forward to explain Chessie is that it is a misidentification of manatees or whales. Another even states that Chessie could be a marine reptile from the Mesozoic era. One hypothesis is that Chassis is a yet to be discovered species of giant marine snake or eel.

Chuchunaa

The chuchunaa, also spelled chuchunya, is another large cryptid hominid seen in northern Asia. The chuchunaa is observed in Russia's harsh environment of Siberia near subpolar temperatures. Even though chuchunaa are seen near the regions where the almasty is seen, many see these creatures as different animals. The chuchunaa is described as a bipedal hominid about 6 feet tall, black fur covering the body except for lighter markings on the limbs and head, a heavy brow ridge, no neck and a human-like face. Tales of the chuchunaa started with the nomadic indigenous cultures of Siberia Yakut and Tungus people which told of a race of violent "people" that could kill anyone that went into their land. Even the tales stated that the chuchunaa would consume human flesh, which is what makes it different from the almasty. Even the USSR made it possible to protect the "people" that lived in Siberia due to the fact that they believed that they were exactly that, people. Later cryptozoologists like Bernard Heuvelmans have suggested that the chuchunaa were not modern humans but a population of extinct humans like Neanderthals and Denisovans, able to survive in the rugged and desolate regions of Siberia. If this were to be true, then the almasty and chuchunaa might be related to each other but because of environmental differences, adapt different morphologies from one another.

Chupacabra

The first sightings of the chupacabra occurred in Puerto Rico in the 1990s. The name means "goat sucker, " in the belief that the creature supposedly attacked goats and chickens by sucking their blood through two puncture wounds in their necks. Witnesses of this animal describe a 3- to 4-foot-tall humanoid creature with large eyes, smooth grey skin and spines down its back that let it fly. Soon enough the attacks and the sightings of this creature stopped but that wasn't the end of the story. Soon an animal called "chupacabra" was attacking animals in Texas. A small town in south Texas called Cuero was an area where local farmers' animals were being attacked by a creature that supposedly drank the blood of its victims and did not eat the flesh like a normal predator. The description of this animal was that it was similar to a coyote in size, but hairless. A woman named Phylis Canion found a dead animal unlike any she had seen before. Ms. Canion sent the carcass of the peculiar animal to scientists who reported that the DNA of the animal were from 2 animals, a coyote and a Mexican wolf which could cause a mutation that caused hairlessness. The supposed chupacabras in Texas are most likely mangy coyotes and probably don't drink the blood of animals. On the other hand, the Puerto Rican chupacabra is thought to be alien in origin or even a genetically engineered creature from a lab on the island.

Crocotta

The crocotta is a cryptid canine seen hundreds of years ago in India and Ethiopia. The legend of the crocotta begins with the lore of the cultures in the regions; tales of a gruesome animal that attacks and eats humans. The first westerner to learn about the creature was the Roman naturalist Pliny, who described the crocotta; "which looks as though it had been produced by the coupling of the wolf and the dog, for it can break anything with its teeth, and instantly on swallowing it digest it with the stomach." This was a great description of the crocotta, as it was believed to be able to eat anything and the crocotta was believed to be something supernatural. Some legends stated that the crocotta could mimic human voices which would draw people into the woods, where it would kill them. Considering these supernatural aspects, some do believe that the crocotta could have been a real animal. There aren't any modern sightings of the crocotta; some have suspected that the crocotta could have been a hyena based on the similarities of the hyena to the crocotta-like the teeth and the ability to eat anything. Even the scientific name for the spotted hyena *crocuta crocuta* was named after the folklore of the crocotta and its description. The crocuta is an example of how a cryptid has turned out to be a real species. This might be applied to many cryptids due to the fact that most are just a species that is yet to be recognized.

Cryptid Felines

This is the name given to the unidentified big cats that are seen all over the world. Sometimes these cats are known as Alien Big Cats, as these species are seen out of their indigenous range or are seen in a region where they are non-native. Some examples are the Beast of Bodmin Moor, black panthers and the blue tiger of India. Descriptions of these animals vary from region to region. Take, for instance, the *panthera atrox* of America, which is seen as a melanistic panther and as a cat which looks like an African lion with a mane, while the blue tiger of India is black and a lighter color of blue in a striped pattern. There are many theories of the origins of these animals. For instance, in the U.K, the felids seen there are believed to be exotic cats released into the country, where they created a small breeding population. n America the felines seen here are believed to be a variety of animals. One theory is that they are melanistic cougars living along the East Coast, another suggests that they are extinct felines from the Pleistocene era like the American lion. In India, the blue tiger is believed to be a melanistic tiger that causes the unique coloration of the animal. For the felines seen in the U.S., it is likely these are a mix of escaped exotics and melanistic cougars. It is also possible that lions seen in North America might be a relict population of Cave Lions. These felines were found from Europe to the Yukon. The other cryptid felines seen across the world are most likely other melanistic cats and escaped exotics.

Con Rit

The Con Rit is an aquatic cryptid seen off the coast of Vietnam. Con Rit means "millipede" in the indigenous dialect which fits due to the description of this aquatic cryptid. Eyewitnesses of the con rit describe an animal about 60 feet long, with a serpentine body composed of large, armored segments about 3 feet long and 2 feet wide, which give the appearance of a centipede, small limbs on both side of each segment which could act as fins, and an insect-like head at the end of the body. The local cultures of Vietnam told tales of a giant sea serpent in South China Sea, where all of the sightings of the con rit occur. Most of the evidence for the con rit is anecdotal except for in 1883 when a so-called "globster" that was believed to be a con rit washed ashore in Hong Gai Bay. The body was missing its head but the body itself was made of armored segments that the individuals there stated rung like metal when struck. The carcass's smell was so horrendous that the body was pulled into the ocean, never to be seen again. The con rit is believed to be a creature that the scientist Bernard Heuvelmans called a "many-finned" sea serpent, one of his hypothetical species of sea serpent. These sea serpents are believed to be *basilosaurus*, an ancient whale. Another explanation for the con rit is that it's a new form of aquatic arthropod that has reached a size not yet recognized by science.

Cuero

The cuero is an unknown aquatic cryptid that is seen throughout western South America. The two countries where the most sightings occur are Argentina and Chile, where the cuero is believed to reside on the bottoms of lakes and rivers. Cuero means "cowhide" which accurately describes the creature; an aquatic animal which is completely flat, red-colored, with circular "teeth" on the circumference of the body, and eyes that protrude out of the body. The cuero is believed to be a predator. When a prey item is unlucky enough to step on the cuero, it wraps around the animal and uses the "teeth " on the outside of the body to consume it. In Argentina, most cuero attacks and sightings occur in Lago Lacar and Lago Nahuelita *(where there are already sightings of a lake monster)*. Both are in the Andes Mountains where many think the most of the cuero are believed to reside. There are a plethora of theories of what the cuero is believed to be. The cryptozoologist Mark Hall believed that the cuero is a giant aquatic scorpion while Karl Shuker believes it could be a species of freshwater jellyfish or stingray. Author Jorge Borges believes that the cuero could be a freshwater species of octopus.

Devil Bird

The Devil Bird is an avian cryptid seen in Sri Lanka. The indigenous tribes of Sri Lanka repeat folklore about a bird that they called a devil bird, as it was thought of a harbinger of death and destruction. The name devil bird was used by colonists who heard legends of this strange bird, which the native tribes Ulama. The tales stated that if an individual heard its haunting cry, that they would later die, a similar belief to legends of the Irish banshee. The description of the devil bird is of a black bird about the size of a large owl, with a wingspan of about 8 feet, an owl-like appearance, and tufts of feathers above the eyes. The ornithologist Chris Primhan believed that the devil bird was a Brown Wood Owl that is indigenous to Sri Lanka, which does have a blood-curdling call like the devil bird. Another ornithologist, William Legge, thought that the creature was a Grey Nightjar in 1880. Even with all of the theories for the true origins of the devil bird, its' identity was not known until 2001. In 2001 what many think the true identity of the devil bird was found. The spot-bellied eagle-owl is the species of bird which many believe to be the devil bird, as its cry is very similar to the ones of the supposed devil bird. The spot-bellied eagle-owl also has large tufts of feathers above its eyes, just as the devil bird is described having.

Devil Dogs

Devil Dogs are another peculiar canine cryptid seen throughout the world. Devil Dogs are similar to other cryptid canines observed, but there appears to be some distinct differences. One difference is that Devil Dogs are thought to be more physical than the hell hounds, which are believed to be metaphysical or spiritual in nature. Devil Dogs are described as a canine about the size of a German shepherd with a very muscular frame and black to grey fur, stocky build, and do look similar to most other canines. These creatures are usually seen in the United States, mostly on the East Coast and the Midwest. Many have made parallels between these creatures and the ghostly black dogs of England and the folklore of the hellhound. Some of the major sightings take place in the American southwest and Midwest. There are many theories of what these animals are. One idea is that they could be misidentifications of known animals and even feral domestic dogs. Another theory states that these animals could be surviving canines that at one time flourished throughout North America like the dire wolf or *borophaginae*, the bone crushing dogs. It is possible that populations of these canines have survived and still persist in the more remote regions of North America.

Devil Monkeys

The devil monkey is another cryptid primate seen in the U.S. The differences of the devil monkey to other cryptid primates in the U.S like bigfoot is that the devil monkey is more anthropoid, rather than the humanoid bigfoot. Devil monkeys are seen primarily in the Midwest and the south of the United States; most sightings of this animal occur near water sources like rivers and swamps. The devil monkey is terrifying due to the description of these primordial primates. The description of the devil monkey is of a primate about 6 to 7 feet long and 5 feet at the shoulder, long black fur, a monkey-like face, long nails, a bushy tail, long canine teeth, and body shape like that of a baboon. The devil monkey is believed to be a very aggressive animal as there are anecdotal references to these animals attacking people in the past and some even say these creatures are responsible for killing livestock. Some sightings have suggested that these animals travel in troops, as they are sometimes seen in groups. Similar to bigfoot it is believed that these creatures use waterways in order to travel. Devil monkeys are a peculiar cryptid because the only known primates in North America were small and very basal. It is possible that these primates were able to survive and evolve into what we now know as devil monkeys, but the lack of fossil evidence might not back up these claims. The true identity of the devil monkey might be an enigma that we might never solve.

Didi

The didi is an unknown bigfoot-like creature that is seen in northern South America. This cryptid is primarily spotted in the countries of Guyana, Columbia and Brazil where there are thick jungles for the didi to live. Unlike other cryptid primates seen in South America, the didi is not believed to be arboreal like the mono grande of Central America. The didi is believed to live on the ground and adapted to that environment. The first people to tell tales of the didi were from the indigenous cultures of South America but the first westerners to hear about the legends of the didi were the Conquistadors from Spain. They described the didi of a human-like primate about 5 to 6 feet tall, covered with long red fur and tailless. Some have even made the idea that this could be the same creature as the De Loys ape which was killed in the area. Even though the didi featured in the folklore of Central America for centuries, there are no known modern sightings of the didi. Most think that the didi could be related to the other unknown primates of South America, like the duende of Belize, the mapinguari of Brazil, the sisemite of Central America and the mono grande of Central America. The primary theory for where these creatures came from is that either they are North American bigfoots which have migrated south and adapted to the change in environment; or that they are unknown forms of primates which have evolved in South America's isolation.

Dobhar-chu

This creature has the appearance of a hybrid between a canine and an otter; and is seen in the myriad of lochs in Ireland. The word dobhar-chu means "water hound" which is what many of the people of Ireland believe it to be. The dobhar-chu is a semiaquatic mammal seen in the lochs of Ireland; it is even nicknamed the Irish crocodile even though it has no reptilian features. The description of the dobhar-chu is of a mammalian creature with the head of an otter, a long body with brown fur, four webbed feet on each leg and a long strong tail. The dobhar-chu is believed to be a very territorial creature based on the belief that any individuals that get too close to a body of water that has dobhar-chu in it could be attacked. A 1700s burial stone describes a story of a woman who was washing clothes near a loch when she was suddenly attacked by a pair of dobhar-chu which killed her, before her husband scared away the ferocious creatures. This story makes many believe that the dobhar-chu could be a very dangerous animal. Many do think that the dobhar-chu is a carnivore that eats fish and other aquatic animals in the waters of Ireland. There are not many sightings of this creature in recent times, which makes many believe this creature is now extinct or very rare. What the dobhar-chu is believed to be is an unknown species of otter indigenous to Ireland.

Dover Demon

The Dover Demon was an unidentified animal seen in Dover, Massachusetts in 1977. The story starts with several teens driving near Dover, who saw a peculiar animal in the local woods. The sightings only occurred for two days, April 21 and 22. The witnesses of the Dover Demon were William Bartlett, John Baxton, and Abby Brabham; all between the ages of 17 and 15. All of them described the creature in the same way; a humanoid animal with a large head, small body compared to the head, white to cream colored skin and deep red eyes. Many authorities believed that the teens were lying about the sightings or was a simple misidentification of a known animal. Even with those explanations, others have their own theories of what the Dover Demon was. One theory speculates that the Diver Demon was an extraterrestrial, based on the large head and small body and that the creature was seen only for about two days. Another theory states that it could be only one of many strange occurrences that happen in the area. Dover is in an area called the Bridgewater Triangle, which has had a large number of UFO sightings, cryptid sightings and strange magnetic phenomena that could explain the Dover Demon. It is possible that the Dover Demon is yet another mystery of the Bridgewater Triangle that might never be truly solved.

Duende

The duende, also spelled dwendi, is a being whose origin lies in the folklore of the cultures of Belize and other regions of South America. The word duende is derived from the word for "dwarf" which is what many think the creature is. The duende is sometimes considered the South American version of the European elves and fairies. Even though the duende is seen in a spiritual sense most of the time, there is still a physical aspect to them. Similar to the alux of the Aztecs the duende is believed to be a race of little people in the jungle. Most of the stories of the duende state that they are very human-like but without any outward technology like fire-making or tool creation. Later researchers think that the duende was not a spiritual creature at all but a physical animal that lives in the jungles of Belize. The description of the duende is of a bipedal humanoid creature, covered with red to black fur, short fur with longer on the head, 3 to 4 feet tall, long arms and legs, a yellow pigment to the skin under the fur and pointed heels like many other small unknown small primates seen across the world. Many think the duende is an animal that the cryptozoologist Ivan T Sanderson calls "proto-pygmies" due to their short stature. Some have suggested that the duende is a creature which could be similar to the agogwe of Africa and the alux of Mexico. Most other proto-pygmies are hypothesised to be relic hominid species, but this is unlikely. It might be possible the duende is a smaller for of bigfoot or a whole new form of simian.

Ebu-gogo

The ebu-gogo is a cryptid primate seen in Flores, Indonesia. The tales of the ebu-gogo start with the oral folklore of the Nage people of central Flores, where the name ebu-gogo translates to "granny glutton". The name is due to the fact that the ebu-gogo is said to be a race of people that live in the forest and would steal food from the Nage. The description of the ebu-gogo is of a humanoid primate about 4 to 5 feet tall, bipedal, long matted fur that covers the body, long muscular arms that allow the ebu-gogo to have the ability to have an arboreal and terrestrial existence. The Nage people's stories relate that the ebu-gogo are extinct, as they killed them all because they would steal their children to consume them as food. The Nage killed the ebu-gogo in a cave when they used fire to suffocate them. Many think that the ebu-gogo were simply a legend to scare children until in 2003 when a new discovery was made in Flores. The discovery was a new species of human named *Homo-floresiensis* which many call the "Hobbit". These humans were only about 3 to 4 feet tall, yet morphologically very similar to modern humans. It is believed that these humans were around the same intelligence of modern humans and did use tools. These "Hobbits" were around during the same time as Homo-sapiens being on Flores. This might show that the ebu-gogo were surviving populations of *Homo floresiensis* or at least a cultural memory of the real jungle hobbits.

Emela-ntouka

This large cryptid was seen in the Likouala Swamp of Central Africa, the same region where there are many other cryptid sightings. This is a very large animal, according to witnesses and legends describing it as about the size of an elephant or a large rhino. The name emela-ntouka means "killer of elephants" in the Lingala language. The indigenous peoples think that the emela-ntouka kills elephants and other large fauna species which come into its territory. The description of the emela-ntouka is of an elephant-sized animal with grey to brown skin, a powerful tail with four strong legs with short nails like a rhino, and a large horn which protrudes out of the animal's snout. There are many theories of where the emela-ntouka came from and what it is. A major one was proposed by Roy Mackal; the emela-ntouka is a surviving dinosaur called a *ceratopsian*. This is different from the natives' stories, who do not describe the animal as reptilian but more like a mammal. It is likely that the stories of the emela-ntouka were misconstrued in order to help with the erroneous idea of a surviving population of dinosaurs living in the Congo. It is most likely that, as there haven't been sightings of this creature since the 1950s, that it's just a cultural memory. Rhinos did at one time roam the areas around the Congo so the emela-ntouka might be a representation of the natives who remember seeing these animals.

Fiji Mermaid

Even though the Fiji Mermaid was a hoax, the legend does have some very helpful lessons. The hoax began in 1842 when the famous showman P.T Barnum demonstrated an oddity that was a creature called the "Fiji Mermaid." An aquatic creature supposedly found near the island of Fiji. People from across the country went to see the animal that Barnum said was a real-life mermaid. The creature was about 3 feet long, a mummified human-like head with small human-like arms emerging from the torso, a fish-like tail with scaly skin and fin along the back. Due to the workmanship of the creature, it made may believe that the animal was real. The exhibit was so lucrative that many other sideshows tried to repeat the Fiji Mermaid, but none were as great as the original mermaid. Later it was demonstrated that the Fiji Mermaid was a hoax, a chimera created from the parts of many animals. The Fiji Mermaid was made with the head and upper torso of a monkey sewed to the lower body of a fish, which together created the appearance of a mermaid. Later many cryptozoologists use the Fiji Mermaid as a lesson that not everything is as it seems. There are always hoaxes so a researcher cannot believe everything that they see and hear. A skeptical mind is always healthy in this profession – as long as the skepticism doesn't become cynicism.

Ryan Edwards

Flathead Lake Monster

The Flathead Lake Monster is an aquatic cryptid seen in Montana's Flathead Lake. Flathead Lake is the largest freshwater lake in the U.S.; being about 28 miles long and 16 miles wide, to a depth of about 370 feet. The description of the Flathead Lake Monster is of an aquatic animal, believed to be a reptile with a long serpentine body about 20 to 40 feet long with brownish to green colored skin and a snake-like head. The indigenous Native American tribes told legends of a large creature living in the lake. Later white settlers came to the area and saw the same creature. The first recorded sighting occurred in 1889 when a man on a steamboat saw a large unknown moving object in the lake. He described a large snake-like creature, coming straight for his boat. After that sighting there were many more, so that people were convinced that there was an unknown animal in the lake. Some have suspected that the creature could be a misidentification of debris in the water or even a large fish called a sturgeon. Other researchers think that the creature could be a new species of fish or aquatic snake. Another likely explanation for the Flathead Lake Monster is a yet-to-be-discovered species of giant eel.

Flatwoods Monster

The Flatwoods Monster is a very peculiar creature seen in West Virginia in 1952. The story of the Flatwoods Monster starts with three children: brothers Edward and Fred May, and their friend Tommy Hyer. The boys saw a strange object in the skies over Flatwoods, West Virginia. They stated that an object they believed to be a UFO landing in a local farm. The boys and went back to gather a group of friends. They all went to the farm to see what the object was, until they saw a peculiar creature in the area of the UFO. The group came upon a creature that they described as an 8-foot-tall humanoid figure, completely black except for two round red glowing eyes, a large, elongated head, two large arms which protruded out of the body, a large frill-like object behind the head, with what appeared to be a long skirt-like garment that gave the thing an appearance of floating above the ground. A strange sulfur-smelling gas also was either emitted by or surrounded the creature. The party of eyewitnesses soon left the area due to fright and the strange smelling gas. The creature has never been seen again, though it is a large part of local folklore and legends. Many have suspected that the Flatwoods Monster, like the Dover Demon, is an extraterrestrial due to the sighting of the UFO at the same time and place. Other researchers have suggested that the Flatwoods Monster was nothing but the misidentification of a large owl by frightened children.

Flying Humanoids

These aerial cryptids are seen all over the world. But most sightings occur in the U.S. and Mexico. It appears that there are 2 types of flying humanoids seen in the U.S. The first is of a humanoid but with a pair of leathery wings protruding out of the creature's back. The description is of a humanoid figure about 5 to 7 feet tall, with bat-like wings which span about 10 to 18 feet, white to cream-colored skin, muscular legs and arms, and a very horrid face that has soul-piercing eyes. These are seen mostly in the south of the U.S from the Appalachian Mountains to the American southwest. The second type of flying humanoid is of a humanoid figure with the ability to float above the ground without wings. These are described as a human figure about 6 feet tall with no particular protrusions. These are seen primarily in Mexico and the Southwest of the U.S. These creatures are violent; some anecdotal sightings state that they even attack people. These are believed to be a form of able to fly through extraterrestrial technology. The locals of Mexico call these creatures "bruja" which means "witch" in Spanish because these creatures have the ability to fly. Personally, I think that flying humans are very unlikely, based on the lack of evolutionary precedent for such a species. There are no known vertebrates with six limbs; all vertebrates have four limbs; a tetrapod. This might demonstrate that flying humanoids are more paranormal or extraterrestrial in origin.

Fouke Monster

The Fouke Monster is a bigfoot-like cryptid seen in Arkansas. The Fouke Monster is named after the town of Fouke, Arkansas, where the first sightings of this creature started. The Fouke Monster sightings began in the early 1970s when several area locals saw a peculiar animal, which was blamed for the depredation of livestock in the area. The creature was described as bigfoot-like, but only about 6 to 8 feet tall with long black fur. Footprints found in the area were said to have about 3 to 5 toes on each foot. One major thing that separates the Fouke Monster from the bigfoot seen in other areas of the country is that this animal was described as being much more violent. In 1971, a man named Bobby Ford was attacked by an animal that was believed to be the beast. The Fouke Monster was so renowned that in 1972, the film called *The Legend of Boggy Creek* was created as a semi-factual documentary of the creature that was seen in the area of Boggy Creek, a swamp close to Fouke. Soon enough, the sightings and attacks stopped, leaving a town that was never the same. Fouke, Arkansas, was put on the map thanks to the creature and the movie, but many still wondered what the creature was. Some think that the creature was a bigfoot or an unknown primate called napes which are more ape-like. The discrepancies between the Fouke Monster and Sasquatch might be due to it being a regional morph, adapted to its environment and possible inbreeding.

Gambo

This could be one of the most famous globsters in history. The story starts on June 12, 1983, on Bungalow Beach in Gambia, Africa. On that day a young man named Owen Burnham found a mysterious aquatic animal washed up on the shore. The native people were going to sell the creature as an oddity, but Owen was able to stop them and was able to see the creature for himself. It was an animal 15 feet long with smooth skin, with a brown coloration on the top and a white belly, a head which resembled a dolphin's but with no blowhole, four flippers and tail that measure about 5 feet long each with no flukes or mammalian qualities. The other individuals at the location said that the peculiar creature was a dolphin, based on the smooth skin and flippers. Later the carcass was buried, and the incident almost forgotten until the cryptozoologist Karl Shuker heard about the creature. Shuker disagreed with the idea that the creature was a dolphin, as it didn't have a blowhole. He thought that it was an extinct marine reptile named a *pliosaur*. He came to this conclusion, based on the *pliosaurus* had four flippers, a tail, and a crocodile-like head. These are almost the exact descriptors for gambo. It is possible that gambo was a carcass of *pliosaur* that has somehow survived in the deep oceans off the Atlantic till this day.

Gazeka

The gazeka is a large mammalian cryptid seen in Papua New Guinea. The legend of the gazeka begins with the indigenous populations of New Guinea telling tales of a large animal, similar to a giant pig or tapir, living deep in the mountains. This legend spread with British explorers that came to Papua New Guinea who heard legends of this animal and even found evidence for the existence of the creature. The English explorer K A W Moncton found large footprints on Mount Albert Edward, belonging to a large mammalian animal whose identity is still unknown. The description of the gazeka is of a mammal about 10 feet long and 6 feet at the shoulder, a large body with brown fur and a strange proboscis-like snout which gives it the appearance of the tapir, which are indigenous to South America and Southeast Asia, or a large pig. The sightings of the gazeka primarily occur on the Owen Stanley Range of southern Papua New Guinea. Evidence for the existence of the gazeka was found in 1962 when ancient carvings of a large animal that inhabited the area match the description given for the gazeka. Bernard Heuvelmans theorized that the gazeka is an extinct marsupial named a *diprotodon* that once lived in Australia. The *diprotodon* had the appearance of a giant wombat, about the size of a cow, though there were smaller subspecies.

Giant Bears

A giant bear is an example of a regular animal but of abnormally large proportions. These animals are seen primarily in the higher latitudes of North America and Asia. In the U.S most of the sightings and attacks of these bears occur in Alaska and the northern parts of Canada. These bears are usually seen when outdoorsmen and hunters go into the most remote regions of the U.S and Canada and see these large animals or on hunting trips and kill animals that are simply gigantic. These animals are described as resembling regular grizzly or black bears but are simply huge, with some being about 12 to 20 feet long from muzzle to the tail and truly gigantic heads. There are many instances of giant bears in history, the most famous are the Bergman's Bear of Russia and the Macfarlane's Bear of Canada. Some even think that these could be holotypes of a new species of bear. These animals are so large that some researchers think that these bears could be examples of extinct bear species which once lived in North America. In the Pleistocene epoch a species named the short-faced bear roamed the plains and forest of North America. This bear was truly gigantic, being 7 foot tall at the shoulder and possibly reaching half a ton in weight. It is possible that this real-life monster has been able to survive in the farthest reaches of the great north. It is also possible that these giant bears being sighted are just regular grizzlies and black bears. but thanks to genetic mutations have reached sizes not yet expected from their species.

Giant Eels

These cryptids are another instance of a regular animal achieving an irregular size. The sightings of these aquatic giants occur mostly in lakes which have averagely low temperatures like the lake of Canada, where most of the sightings of these gigantic eels occur. In Canada there is an extensive history of giant eels seen in their local lakes and other sources of water. The indigenous tribes of the area tell legends of "giant water serpents." These stories aren't describing snakes but eels that are of a giant size. The common description of these animals is of a long animal, about 8 to 20 feet long with coloration from black to grey smooth skin and no discernable fins. These animals could be a variety of species. Many point out the conger eel that is found off the shore of North America, the problem is that the conger eel only reaches about 10 feet long. Another candidate is the American eel, which normally reaches only about 4 feet long. One theory is that these animals are known species of eels, growing to the length that witnesses see. These sightings occurring in colder lakes might back up their existence, as it has been shown that species in colder water can grow larger than ones in warmer water. Many speculate that these eels could explain the sightings of lake monsters in many lakes in Canada like the Ogopogo of Lake Okanagan, the Winnepogo of Lake Winnipeg, and the menagerie of other lake monsters seen in Canada.

Giant Snakes

These are yet another instance of a known animal reaching unknown, gigantic sizes. These animals are seen all over the world but one of the most famous examples of a giant snake is the giant anaconda of South America. This particular cryptid is seen in the Amazon jungle of Brazil where there is a population of the already large anaconda which reaches lengths of about 17 feet, but the giant anaconda has been said to reach lengths of about 160 feet long. The legend of the giant anaconda began when westerners came into South America and heard tales of these giants from the indigenous population. Later Spanish missionaries and explorers who went into the jungles of Brazil reported their own sightings of the animal. The creature was believed to be so large that it could eat bulls by just swallowing them. Many cryptozoologists believe that this animal could have a high possibility of existing, thanks to the remote regions offering a high variety of food sources and sheltering habitat. Even though the giant anaconda is the most famous of all the unknown giant snakes, it is far from being the only one. There is a plethora of cultures around the world which have a folklore of giant snakes. One is the naga of the Hindu and Buddist religion, which could be real creatures. These species might be snakes of a known species which are larger than ordinary specimens or they might be entirely new species. The giant anaconda, for instance, might be a population of a giant snake called the *titanoboa* which reportedly reached up to 60 feet in length.

Giant Spiders

Arachnophobia is the fear of spiders. Many people are afraid of regular spiders but just imagine meeting one of these creepy creatures the size of a small dog. These giant arachnids are seen globally, but they are seen primarily in tropical environments. The most sightings occur in South America and Africa, along with some sightings in the Middle East. The common description of these creatures is of an animal that resembles a tarantula but with the diameter of about 5 feet across. In South America the giant spiders seen are so large that the indigenous population describe the creatures being able to carry off dogs and even small children. The natives are so afraid that they make their huts above the ground in order to protect themselves from these spiders. In Africa the sightings of giant spiders describe a creature that also resembles a giant tarantula. These animals were first seen by English missionaries and explorers who went into the remote jungles of Africa. In the Middle East, the creatures seen are animals known as camel spiders that are actually not spiders at all but an arachnid known as a *solifugae* whose name means "those who flee from the sun" in Latin. American soldiers in the Middle East came back with stories of giant camel spiders that could eat dogs. In Earth's past there have been giant spiders about half again the size of these seen now. It is possible that natural history has repeated itself and has created spiders the size of their giant predecessors a millennia ago.

Giant Squid

This is an instance of an animal that was once considered only mythical, but which has later been proven to be real. The giant squid also known as *Architeuthis* is a colossal cephalopod that lives in the inky depths of the oceans across the world. The legend of the giant squid started with sailors that went across the ocean and told stories of a giant animal that attacked their ships while at sea. These sailors would describe the creature as a large squid about 40 feet long, with two large arms and about ten smaller tentacles which had the ability to grab sailors. This is seen to be very similar to the legend of the kraken of the northern Atlantic Ocean. These tales were viewed as just folklore, until in 2002 a video image showing a giant squid was made off the coast of Japan. Since then, the giant squid has been proven to be a real species and not at all folkloric; even though the many stories of squid attacking sailors could have just been fictional stories made from having seen such creatures when they come to the surface. Bodies of these animals have also washed ashore on many beaches across the world. Necropsies of these animals have demonstrated that these animals are very large and probably very intelligent. Most cryptozoologists think of the giant squid as a sign of hope for some of the so-called fictitious and mythical animals in the world being based in real biological species. The existence of giant squids strongly suggests that there are discoveries yet to be made in our world.

Globsters

This is the name for any biological tissue that washes on a beach whose origin of species is unknown. The cryptozoologist Ivan T. Sanderson was the individual that created the name for this phenomenon. There has been a plethora of instances of unknown carcasses being found across the globe; one of the first is the Tasmanian Blob that was found in 1960. These blobs are described in many ways but most of these carcasses are said to look very similar to long-necked animals like *plesiosaurs* and *pliosaurs* and other extinct marine reptiles. Many have speculated that these unknown carcasses are instances of dead sea serpents that are now decaying on the beach and there are other researchers that think that these carcasses could be dead and decaying giant squids. The true identity of these animals is hard to identify due to the amount of decay that the body is under and many of these are just what the name describes, they are just a mound of organic tissue that could have come from any known or unknown pelagic organism. Many zoologists and biologists have written off all instances of globsters as just decaying whale blubber or as a known organism like an oarfish, which many examples have proved to be, but there are a small number of globsters that cannot be explained so easily. These globsters might actually be remains of unknown marine animals.

Goatmen

This is a name used for a group of very peculiar cryptids seen in the United States. The name comes from witnesses describing these creatures as a mix of goat and human, similar to the being Pan from Greek mythology. Most of the sightings of these strange ungulates occur along the East Coast of the U.S and the Appalachian Mountains. Two particular instances are the Sheepsquatch of West Virginia, and the Popelick Monster of Kentucky. The common description of these animals is of a bipedal creature about 6 to 9 feet tall, with white to black fur covering the body, horns, and hoofed goat-like legs. If the description of this creature is to be taken as reality it can't possibly exist. The goatman could be an example of a cultural idea that has formed into a perceived reality. Due to the high frequency of reports and mentions of the goatman this has caused many to think they are real. If an individual has a pre-existing notion that this being exists, then they will perceive it in their own reality. This phenomenon occurs frequently in cryptozoology and can help show how misidentification can happen. Individuals can speak of a creature as if it is real even if it isn't, based on that in their own reality and psyche it does. This does hinder true scientific research into this field. Most likely, what people perceive as a goatman is a misidentification of a known species or another cryptid such as bigfoot. So the real goatman's home isn't our woods, it's the human psyche.

Grassman

The grassman is a regional name used for a bigfoot-like cryptid seen in Ohio. The name grassman comes from hut-like structures made from long grasses. They are believed to be made by the Grassman which implies the intelligence of a great ape. Known great apes like gorillas and chimps are known for making nests themselves. These highly intricate structures show that mere children can't make these and there are no known animals in Ohio create such a nest. The description of the grassman is similar to other bigfoot-like creatures seen in the U.S.; a large bipedal humanoid with long black to red fur, long arms, large feet and very human-like in appearance. Most sightings occur in Ohio, especially in Salt Fork State Park, sometimes called the Sasquatch Triangle for the number of sightings in the area. Even though it goes by another name the grassman is not another species akin to bigfoot, they are bigfoot themselves. The name grassman is just the name used for the bigfoots seen in that particular region, it is not a different species of animal. This occurs across the U.S where there is a plethora of different names used for bigfoot and bigfoot-like animals for instance the Fouke Monster of Arkansas, and the Skunk Ape of Florida. These are just colloquial names for the same species we know as bigfoot or sasquatch. A slight disparity in physical attributes of these creatures might just be an example of a regional morph of bigfoot that have adapted to their own region.

Grootslang

The grootslang is a cryptid seen in Africa. Tales of the grootslag started with the oral folklore of South Africa which has stories of a very peculiar creature. The tale goes that the gods created a creature and soon realized that they had made a terrible mistake in doing so. So, the gods split the grootslang into parts, making the first elephants and snakes, but one grootslang was able to escape and recreate the species. Soon the grootslang made its home in a local cave, lakes, and swamps. Grootslang translates to "big snake" from some of the first colonist's original description of an animal with the body of an elephant and tail of a snake. Soon British and Dutch colonists came to Africa and heard legends of the creature but stated that they saw a very different animal. They described a giant aquatic snake about 20 to 30 feet long, similar to the nguma-monene. Soon the colonists correlated the animal they were seeing with the grootslang of the original legend. Many cryptozoologists believe that the grootslang is an instance of a surviving dinosaur in Africa. This cryptid is believed to possibly be a *ceratopsian* like the emela-ntouka. While others think it could be a misidentification of pythons or other large reptiles like the Nile Monitor. It's very possible that the grootslang might be an unknown species of giant python that has made its home in the waterways of South Africa.

Gunni

The gunni is a peculiar animal seen in Australia. The legend started in Victoria, Australia, where a creature like none never seen before was found dead. Soon the body was put on display and named the gunni. The description of the gunni is of a wombat with the antlers of a deer on its head. Soon the locals said there was a history of these creatures; in the 1860s prospectors saw these creatures in the area. Many authorities believed that these tales were hoaxes or caused by alcohol. Soon after that, the gunni were just thought of as an urban myth … until there were several sightings of a peculiar creature matching the description of the gunni. One of the most well-known sightings was in 1999 when Flak Murphy claimed to see a gunni near Marysville, Victoria. He described the creature as being about the size of a wombat with brown fur and large antlers on its head. Soon it was proven that the gunni was nothing but a hoax, one created by a few individuals to try to play a trick. Think of the gunni as similar to the jackalope of the U.S. The gunni and jackalope help show how there are a myriad of hoaxes and tricksters in this field. In the world of cryptozoology, it is hard to walk the tightrope of belief and science but it is one that still can be crossed. Through analysis and science creatures whose existence is just believed and not known can still be proven. Also the ones whose existence is false can also be shown to not have existed in the first place.

Hadjel

The hadjel also known as the Ennedi tiger is a cryptid feline seen in Africa. The Hadjel is seen in the country of Chad in Western Africa. There are a myriad of names for this creature, from Gassingram to Vossoko which describe a feline that originates from the tales of the Zagaoua people. The indigenous tribes state that there are two different types of hadjel, one which inhabits the mountains and is called the hadjel and a water dwelling one, the dilali or mamaime. The description of the mountain dwelling hadjel is of a feline larger than a lion with reddish to brown fur, long claws, short, bobbed tail, and long canines that protrude out of both sides of the mouth. While the description of the water dwelling hadjel is of a mammalian animal bigger than a lion, also with brown to orange fur and long protruding canines, with reports describing a long tail. The natives are very afraid of this creature due to the sheer size of it and there are several stories of these animals attacking people and even whole villages. There are several theories of what the hadjel is, some have even speculated that they could be misidentifications of lions. The cryptozoologist Karl Shuker theorizes that it is a species of saber-toothed cat. Saber-toothed cats did evolve in Africa and there were several species found there. It is possible that one of the many species of saber tooths from the Pleistocene survive alongside the other megafauna of Africa till this day.

Hellhounds

Even though many think of these creatures as just fiction this might not be exactly the truth. The "hellhound" is thought to have originated from the Judeo-Christian religion, but tales of astral dogs believed to have originated from a supernatural source have persisted for thousands of years. One of the first instances is the god Bau of Mesopotamia, believed to be a canine being or at least half dog. Another instance is the Egyptian god Anubis, the god of the afterlife. These demonstrate that most religions and mythologies of the world have legends of large demonic dogs, which are described in very similar ways. Many cryptozoologists believe that these animals were created thanks to real-life canines. In modern-day America there are several instances of individuals seeing large unknown dogs that they state are similar to the biblical hellhounds. The main characteristic that separates those animals from the other cryptid canines seen across the world is that these creatures are described as having glowing red eyes. This causes many to think that these creatures are not physical beings but are more spiritual in nature. The hard part about researching these creatures is that once something falls out of the physical world and lands in the more spiritual one, it is no longer cryptozoology. Even with the spiritual connotation. it is still possible that these sightings might be due to people seeing other unknown canines like devil dogs and bipedal canines.

Hibagon

The hibagon is a cryptid primate seen in Japan. The hibagon is seen in the forests on Mount Hiba in the Hiroshima Prefecture, in the Hiba-Dogo-Taishaku Quasi National Park. The hibagon is very similar to other unknown primates seen across the world like the bigfoot of the United States and the yeti of the Himalayas. One difference is that the hibagon is described as more ape-like that bigfoot and other large unknown primates. The description of the hibagon is of a semi-bipedal primate, about 5 feet tall, with red to black fur, a brown-colored face with intelligent eyes, a snubbed nose, triangular heels, and a prognathic face, more like apes and monkeys. The history of sightings of the hibagon is actually really recent, with the first documented sightings occurring in the 1970s. There were a large number of sightings of a peculiar simian creature in the area from 1970 to 1982, when the legend of the hibagon started. There were so many sightings that in 1972 the Kobe University researched the sightings and sent research teams into the area but didn't find any physical evidence for the Hibagon. The origins of the hibagon is unknown but some think that it is a creature that was created in the atomic bomb dropped on Hiroshima in 1945. Others suspect it's a form of proto-pygmy, which has been able to hide in the forest of Japan for centuries. and has only been seen recently thanks to human encroachment on its territory.

Honey Island Swamp Monster

The Honey Island Swamp Monster is a regional name for a bigfoot-like creature seen in Louisiana. The story of the Honey Island Swamp Monster started with a man named Harlan Ford who stated that he saw a large human-like creature in the bayous in the area of Honey Island. Harlan Ford described the creature as 6 to 8 feet tall, bipedal bigfoot-like creature with long matted black fur covering the body. The most peculiar aspect of the description of the Honey Island Swamp Monster is that it only has three toes on each foot, rather than the usual five toes on bigfoot tracks and the human foot. After Harlan Ford's death, a film which supposedly showed the creature was discovered. The film depicts a bipedal figure walking across the screen behind several trees and foliage. This is one of only two or three pieces of evidence for the creature. Another instance of evidence for the existence of the creature are tracks found by Harlan Ford, which are human-like but tridactyl, only having three toes. The local legend for the origins of the creature is that a circus train crashed and released chimps into the swamp which then interbred with the alligator population, which would be impossible. Most consider it a hoax carried out by Ford, as there are no sightings after the death of Harlan Ford. It is possible that there are bigfoot in that area of Louisiana but the creature known as the Honey Island Swamp Monster is mostly fictitious.

Igopogo

The creature known as Igopogo is a lake monster seen in the Canadian lake of Lake Simcoe in Ontario. The name Igopogo is a play on the cryptid Ogopogo. a creature similar to this one but seen in Lake Okanagan. The description of Igopogo is of a long aquatic animal with a reptile-like serpentine body, dark in color with smooth skin. Another description is of a mammalian animal, pinniped-like with an elongated body and flippers. The sightings of Igopogo can be more believable than other lake monsters due to Lake Simcoe having a surface area of 287 miles and a depth of 135 feet. The tales of the Igopogo started with the indigenous tribes in the area telling tales of a giant animal in the lake. Soon Europeans came to the area and started seeing the creature for themselves. The first modern sighting occurred in 1963, as a witness described an animal similar to a snake swimming in the lake. Most of the sightings of Igopogo occur in Kempenfelt Bay, where a peculiar picture was taken. The image shows two children along the shore and two semicircular hump shapes in the water, which are believed to be the creature. The theories of what Igopogo is numerous. Some think that it could be an unknown species of freshwater pinniped or even a giant unknown eel, like the many other lake monsters seen in Canada.

Iliamna Lake Monster

The Iliamna Lake Monster is yet another lake monster that is seen in North America. This aquatic cryptid is seen in Lake Iliamna, about 150 miles south of Anchorage, Alaska, a lake large enough to hide a monster, covering 1,012.5 square miles in area. The creature is also known as Illie from the local population, the legend of Illie starts long before settlers came into the area. The Native Americans of the area told of a creature in the lake that they called the "jig-ik-nak" which would attack their boats while crossing the lake and would kill their tribe members. Soon the colonists started seeing the creature, but the first documented modern sighting occurred in 1942, when pilots Babe Alyesworth and Bill Hammersley saw what they described as a large grey, blunt-headed fish creature swimming across the lake. That does fit the description of the Iliamna Lake Monster, described as a 15-foot-long creature, white to grey in color, with an elongated body and fins which resemble a fish. A theory of what the creature might be, is an animal known as a *zeuglodon*, a prehistoric cetacean from 40 to 35 million years ago. Another and more likely theory is that the creature is a giant white sturgeon, which does live in Lake Iliamna. White sturgeon can reach lengths up to 14 feet. With the size of Lake Iliamna, they might even reach larger sizes … which would be a truly monstrous fish.

Inkanyamba

The inkanyamba is a lake creature that is seen in Africa. The sightings originated in the South African Kwazulu-Natal Province where most of the sightings occur in the Howick Falls in South Africa. The legend of the inkanyamba starts with the Zulu tribe which told legends of an aquatic serpent with the head of a horse and about 30 or more feet long. Even though most of the sightings occur in Howick Falls there are even more areas of where this creature is seen, for instance it is seen in the Mkomazi and Umgeni Rivers as well as several other lakes and rivers. Some folklorists think that the inkanyamba is not even a physical animal but a supernatural being from the beliefs of the Zulu people that can control the weather. While others do think that the inkanyamba is a physical being due to the description of the animal and the fact that there are eyewitnesses to this creature. The description of the inkanyamba is of a 30-foot-long serpent with a forked tongue with a horse-like head with green scales and no fins. The inkanyamba was not a well-known cryptid until in 1996 when a local newspaper offered a cash reward for any individual that was able to bring photographic evidence of the creature. Two photos were sent but turned out to be hoaxes. One theory of what the inkanyamba is that it is a giant eel or a giant aquatic snake. Others suspect that the inkanyamba could be a giant form of fish whose description and nature has changed over time.

Inzignanin

The inzignanin is an unknown reptilian cryptid seen in the United States. The legend of the inzignanin originated with the indigenous tribe of the Carolinas which told tales of lizard-like humanoids that lived in the wilderness. The inzignanin were described as reptilian humanoids about 6 feet tall with green colored skin, tails, and sharp lizard-like teeth. I've included this creature in this book about cryptids not because I think it exists but because this creature is just one of many people call reptilians. The beings known as reptilians have permeated the cultural imagination in recent times thanks to conspiracy theorists and UFO researchers. The name reptilian is used for a group of beings that share both reptile-like and hominid-like traits. These beings supposedly hold a high intelligence and might even have origins from out of this world. The reptilian phenomena in the mainstream have just begun occurring recently, which might demonstrate how a being that originated from our collected cultural imagination has been transformed into perceived reality. People who state they see reptilians are most likely predisposed to seeing them thanks to their belief in them. This is the same phenomenon as the goatman. Since in recent times there are more stories of reptilians, people see them more. This doesn't mean that these creatures are actually real but that thanks to individual beliefs and perception they are real to them. The reptilians are beings of the human imagination, not out in the wilderness.

Irizima

The irizima is a lake monster believed to be a living dinosaur in Africa. Most of the sightings occur in Lake Edward in Uganda and the Democratic Republic of the Congo. Tales of the irizima originated with the indigenous population and legends of a large animal dwelling in local lakes and rivers. The description of the irizima is of an animal larger than a hippo, long neck, black scale-covered skin, with four strong legs and a long tail. Some descriptions state that the irizima has a horn that protrudes out of the snout, similar to the emela-ntouka of the Congo. The irizima is believed to be a semi-aquatic animal, as most sightings occurred in the water, but there have been a small portion of sightings stating that they see the creature walk on land. The similarity in descriptions have caused many to speculate that the irizima could be similar to the mokele-mbembe of the Congo, believed to be a dinosaur. Due to the pure unlikely hood of a surviving non-avian dinosaur living until modern times, it is unlikely the irizima is truly a dinosaur. Most cryptids in this region are believed to be a form of living dinosaur so it's possible the irizima has had the same treatment, even with it not being a dinosaur at all. The identity of the irizima might always be an enigma to the study of cryptozoology.

Isnachi

The isnachi is an unknown primate seen in the Andes Mountains of Peru. Unlike the other cryptid primates seen in the world the isnachi is not believed to be human-like; they are more monkey-like. The description of the isnachi is of an arboreal primate, appearing similar to a spider monkey, but double in size; about 4 feet tall, black to dark brown fur, thick short tail that doesn't appear to prehensile, a muzzle similar to the mandrill of Africa, long canine teeth and long claws. Even with such a frightening description, the isnachi is believed to be a herbivore, consuming wild fruit and shoots from trees. The isnachi is a solitary animal but there are sightings of them moving in troops up to 20 individuals, similar to extant spider monkeys. The local people of the Andes Mountains do believe that the isnachi lives in the mountains, where the human population is greatly reduced. There are no isnachi sightings on record below 1,500 feet in elevation, which suggests the isnachi is an alpine primate. Theories of what the isnachi might be suggest that it is a misidentification of the spectacled bear, even though the distinctive eye rings of the bear is not an aspect of the isnachi. Another theory is that it is an unknown species of monkeys, most likely spider monkeys. It is possible that this species is a large unknown example of spider monkey, which has adapted to an alpine environment in order to hide away from humans and competition from other monkey species found in the lowland jungles.

Issie

Issie is a lake monster that is seen in the Japanese lake of Ikeda. The name Issie comes from an imitation of Nessie the lake monster seen in Scotland. The local origin legend of Issie is that at one point a mare and her foal lived on the score of Lake Ikeda. A samurai stole the foal and the mare, being so desperate for her foal turned herself into a giant aquatic animal to look for her lost offspring. The life in Lake Ikeda doesn't vary a lot due to a decrease in species. The largest known animal in the lake are eels that can grow up to 6 feet long but that is diminutive compared to Issie. The description of Issie is of an aquatic saurian beast that reaches from 16 to 40 feet long with black coloration, humps on its back, serpentine body, and a snake-like head. A small rash of sightings occurred in December of 1978, when an investigator named Tokiashi Matsubara took a picture of a creature in the lake that was serpentine and similar to the description of Issie. Many later researchers think that the picture depicts a giant eel or a misidentification of a log in the water. The final identity of the object in the image is inconclusive. The theories of what Issie is that it is just misidentifying known animals and objects. Another theory is that the creature is a giant eel. It is possible that Issie is a mix of misidentifications and hoaxes in order to bring tourism to the lake.

Ivory-Billed Woodpecker

Unlike most cryptids in this book this creature is a recognized species. The ivory-billed woodpecker is yet another instance of a creature that has been deemed extinct but is still seen sporadically in the modern day, which puts it into the cryptozoological realm, no longer zoological. This large species of woodpecker with red plumage on the head with a striped black and white body that was very striking, it was indigenous to the southern U.S and was declared extinct in the 1960s. The extinction was due to the over hunting perpetrated by humans and a loss of their habitat thanks to logging. The Cuban subspecies of the ivory-billed woodpecker was later declared extinct in the 1990s. Yet, there are still sightings of this bird in the southern United States and Cuba. In 1999 a zoological student believed he saw a pair of ivory-bills in the Louisiana swamps. An investigation into the sighting occurred and was believed to record the distinctive pecking of the bird; most ornithologists think these sounds weren't woodpeckers but actually gunshots in the distance. Another incident occurred in the Big Woods region of Arkansas in 2004, which is where a video was made that supposedly depicts a male ivory-billed woodpecker. In both of those areas it is believed to be a small population of ivory-billed woodpecker. It is possible the ivory-billed woodpecker still exists in the United States and has been able to hide away from the most disruptive species of humans.

Jersey Devil

This aerial cryptid is seen in a large, forested area in the state of New Jersey known as the Pine Barrens in the Warren State Forest. There are a plethora of descriptions of this particular cryptid. One of the most well-known is of a bipedal creature with the body of a kangaroo, a horse-like head with hooves, bat-like wings and glowing eyes. This particular description does not match any known fauna indigenous to the region. With the peculiarity of the description of the creature the origin story is even stranger. The legend states that in the 1700s a woman named Mother Leeds had 12 children and upon news of a 13 pregnancy cursed the child. Once born, the child turned into a horrid, winged creature and escaped into the Pine Barrens. The Devil was primarily just a piece of local folklore until in 1901 when there were hundreds of sightings of the creature, but it was later shown this was due to a hoax by some teenagers and mass hysteria. I personally don't believe in the Jersey Devil as it is described, there isn't any biological or evolutionary precedent for such a creature. I believe the devil is an example of combined characteristics; a single animal made from misidentification of several others. It is possible that sasquatch and thunderbird sightings have influenced the overall appearance of the Jersey Devil. It is also possible that the 1901 hoax has permanently altered the public's perceived appearance of the creature.

Kalanoro

The kalanoro is an unknown human-like primate seen in Madagascar. Most of the indigenous tribes from all over Madagascar tell tales of a race of diminutive people inhabiting the local jungles. The most prevalent description for the kalanoro is of a bipedal humanoid creature about 3 to 5 feet tall with grey fur, pointed heels, human-like face and body. A peculiar aspect to the description of the kalanoro is that the creature is said to have backward facing feet; this characteristic is sometimes shared with the legends of other unknown primates. Many anthropologists think that the kalanoro is just a legend originating from Madagascar, but most researchers think that is unlikely, as tales of the kalanoro are so prevalent. Bernard Heuvelmans thought the kalanoro existed though he said the legends were "fantastic." He theorized that the kalanoro is an animal called an *Archaeolemur* or *Hadropithecu*s. Both species are extinct now. Both were more anthropoid than the description of the kalanoro. This has caused others to suspect this animal might be an early hominid species which found its way to Madagascar. This might be the explanation, as the fossil record has shown the early hominids had the ability to reach islands. Madagascar might be one that they reached and still persist there till this day.

Kappa

The kappa is a reptilian semi-aquatic cryptid seen in Japan. The tales of this creature originated with the folklore of Japan which stated that the kappa is a humanoid creature which dwells in local waterways like rivers and creeks. The kappa was a feared creature, as it was believed that it supposedly drowned children who got too close to the water. Another aspect that was frightening about the kappa is its appearance. The description of the kappa is of a humanoid reptilian creature with the face of a turtle, about 3 to 5 feet tall, skin covered in green scales, webbed feet and hands, a shell on its back and a dip on its head. Legend states that the dip on the kappa's head contains water and if that water is spilled the kappa loses its strength. The belief in the kappa is so strong that in some towns there are firework shows to scare off the kappa. Most think that the kappa is a fictional character, created by individuals who wanted to create a bogey man in order to scare their kids and keep them away from the water. Others think that the kappa is a misidentification of giant salamanders, which are indigenous to the regions where the kappa is seen. Another explanation is that the kappa is an unknown turtle, but due to fear and cultural perception it has been turned into a water monster that is to be feared and avoided at all cost.

Kapre

The kapre is yet another unknown hominid seen in Southeast Asia. The legend of the kapre originated in the folklore of the indigenous populations of the Philippines. Those tales say that the kapre is a huge bipedal human-like creature, dwelling in trees. In some stories, the kapre even have supernatural powers and are more akin to a forest deity. The description of the kapre is of a human-like figure, 6 to 9 feet tall, black to grey fur, long arms with no tail, and human-like face. Most indigenous populations believe that the kapre is an arboreal animal, as most sightings occur when the creature is in the trees. The kapre is said to be a kindly primate; does not interfere with humans and tries to stay away from them. Most think that the kapre is a fictional deity, created in order to protect the trees where they supposedly make their home. There have been sightings from colonists in the area who believed it was a demonic entity. Due to the description many cryptozoologists think that the kapre could have been a real-life animal, similar to the other large unknown hominids seen in Southeast Asia. One theory for the kapre is that it's a new species of monkey, which might display more human characteristics. Another hypothesis states that the kapre might be a population of *homo erectus* that were known to have reached some of the islands in the Southeast Asian archipelago.

Kawekaweau

The kawekaweau is yet another large unknown lizard seen in New Zealand. The kawekaweau originated with the indigenous Maori people of New Zealand, who tell tales of a giant dangerous lizard, dwelling in the local jungles. Most of the sightings occur in the Wapka Ridge region of New Zealand. The description of the kawekaweau is of a gecko-like lizard, red to orange in color, 2 to 4 feet long, with a serrated dorsal crest, and a stripe running down its back. Once Europeans came to New Zealand, they heard from the indigenous populations that the kawekaweau is a dangerous animal but there are no documented sightings from settlers of the kawekaweau. The sightings of the kawekaweau decreased since the 1600s, when settlers first went into New Zealand. There have been some recent sightings of this creature in the 1960s and 1980s. In one sighting, a witness stated that while driving they saw a large lizard, another when a motorist stated they killed a 2-foot-long lizard while driving but the body was never found. Most herpetologists believe that the the kawekaweau is a giant species of gecko called the Delcourt's giant gecko, endemic to New Zealand but believed to be extinct today. This animal might be the basis for the legend of the kawekaweau.

Kikiyaon

The kikiyaon is a large owl-like bird seen in Africa. The kikiyaon is seen primarily in central Zambia where the indigenous population of the Bambara people tell tales of this terrifying bird of prey. The kikiyaon is thought of as a demon or an evil spirit, originating from the forest. The Bambara people believe that the kikiyaon is an omen of bad luck and should be avoided, and if an individual sees the kikiyaon, a person around them will die. The description of the kikiyaon is of a bird with a 7-to-9-foot wingspan, with an owl-like body, brown to grey colored feathers, a short tail, and a rounded face similar to an owl. The most frightening feature are the large talons that can be used to kill and capture food. One sign that the kikiyaon is in the area is the unique vocalization that it makes. The call is described as an owl-like hoot but much lower, indicating that it is originating from a much larger bird than any indigenous owl species. Most researchers think that the kikiyaon could be an unknown large species of owl. The largest known owl in Africa is the Verreaux Eagle Owl which has a wingspan reaching about 4 to 5 feet wide and is native to Sub-Saharan Africa. Some think this could be the kikiyaon, or even that the kikiyaon is a new species of owl which is larger than any known owl species.

Ryan Edwards

Kongamato

The kongamato is an unknown aerial reptile seen in the remote regions of Western Africa. The kongamato is seen in the Jiundu Swamp in the Congo where the indigenous cultures have been telling stories of the kongamato for centuries. The name translates to "the overwhelmer of boats," as the kongamato usually attack when people are in their canoes. The description of the kongamato is of a reptile with a wingspan from 7 to 12 feet wide, red in color, with two leathery wings, a small body with a tail, a small head, and razor-sharp teeth and claws. When the first Westerners came to the Congo the natives told legends of the kongamato which the Westerners thought of as simple birds. This was until later researchers and cryptozoologists went to the areas the kongamato are seen and showed the witnesses pictures. The researchers show pictures of known birds, which they state they are not the kongamato. Then, they show them pictures of a *pterosaur* in which they state that is the kongamato. Many speculate on the possibility of the kongamato being a surviving population of *pterosaurs*, which have survived their extinction 65 million years ago. This created the hypothesis that the kongamato are *pterosaurs* that have been able to survive in the jungles of Zambia and the Congo. Another more probable explanation is a misidentification of known large bat species or a yet to be discovered large bat species. This might demonstrate a correlation with the kongamato, and another winged cryptid seen in this region of Africa, the olitiau.

Koolakamba

The koolakamba is yet another large unknown primate seen in Africa, but the distinguishing aspect of the koolakamba and other large cryptid primates seen in the world is that it is described as more anthropoid than humanoid. This cryptid primate is seen in Western Africa in the countries of Cameroon to Gabon. There are also sightings of the koolakamba in the Republic of the Congo. The indigenous populations that first encountered the koolakamba believed that they were a hybrid of chimps and gorillas. The name koolakamba originated from the vocalization the creature made that sounded like "kooloo kooloo." The koolakamba is described as a primate that resembles a more muscular chimpanzee, with long black fur, a flatter non-prognathic face, and long arms. The koolakamba are seen in the high-altitude forests of Western Africa where they are believed to live solitary lives, unlike other great apes indigenous to Africa. One of the first Europeans to describe and see the koolakamba was the Frenchman named Paul Du Chaillu, who collected a specimen of a supposed koolakamba. Most researchers believe this creature to be a hybridization between chimp and gorilla. The real explanation for the koolakamba might have already been discovered. In 2003 the bili ape was discovered, a new subspecies of chimpanzee which are much larger and have a different morphology than other chimps. These apes were called "lion killers" due to aggression. This ape is most likely the scientific basis for the koolakamba.

Kraken

In the Northern Atlantic there are stories of a giant cephalopod called the kraken. The story of the kraken originated with maritime sailors who traveled through the Northern Atlantic and returned with unbelievable stories. The sailors claimed the kraken was a giant octopus-like being, able to sink a ship with its huge tentacles, which were able to wrap around the ship and pull it down into the water. Other stories claimed the kraken was so large it was able to create a whirlpool by diving under the water, which could destroy entire ships. Other stories said that the kraken had the ability to reach its tentacles above the water in order to pull sailors off their ships. The description of the kraken is of a giant octopus or squid, 30 to 80 feet long, red in color, with a large body and 8 long tentacles which protrude from the body, a central beak which allowed that creature to feed, two large eyes and suckers on each of the limbs. Most researchers thought that the kraken was a fictional animal created by sailors to make their adventures even more fantastical. This notion was held until the giant squid was discovered. Most cryptozoologists think that the kraken was a giant squid itself. Others have hypothesized that the kraken isn't a giant squid but a species of giant octopus. The behavior of the kraken attacking ships is most likely false, as are the larger size estimates for the kraken. The kraken demonstrates how a once unbelievable animal can be proven to exist, based on a real biological animal, thanks to scientific discoveries.

Kumi Lizard

The kumi lizard is a colossal lizard indigenous to New Zealand. The kumi lizard was first seen by the indigenous people, the Maori who told stories of its size and ferocity. The description of the kumi lizard is of a monitor lizard, but of one about 5 to 7 feet long with scale covered skin, green in color and with long claws. One of the first Westerners that wrote of the kumi lizard was Robyn Gosset, about Maori encountering this beast. Many mistake the kumi lizard to another cryptid reptile, the kawekaweau, also seen in the area. The kumi lizard is believed to be arboreal, spending most of its time in the trees, a differentiation between the primarily terrestrial kawekaweau. Most cryptozoologists think the kumi lizard is an extinct reptile called *megalania*. This was a 20-foot-long monitor lizard indigenous to Pleistocene-era Australia. Some have theorized that this animal moved to modern-day New Zealand and has been able to survive in the remote regions of the country. Another more probable explanation is that the kumi lizard is a mislocated giant monitor lizard like the komodo dragon or Nile monitor, able to survive in the wilds of New Zealand. Some even think that the kumi lizard is another yet-to-be discovered species of giant gecko like the kawekaweau.

Kussie

Kussie, also spelled Kusshii, is a lake monster sighted in Japan. This particular cryptid is seen in Lake Kussharo on the Japanese island of Hokkaido. This lake has an area of 30.6 miles and a depth of 387 feet, large enough area to hide a yet-to-be-recognized reptilian creature. Sightings of the Kussie date back to the 1970s when the first sightings started to occur. The name Kussie was created from emulating the name Nessie, used for the lake monster seen in Loch Ness. Some of the first sightings occurred in 1973 when many local individuals observed a peculiar creature in the lake. The description of Kussie is of a creature about 50 to 60 foot long, brown-colored skin, a large body with flippers, a long neck with a small tail, a horse-like head and a ridge down its back similar to a crocodile. One aspect of the Kussie that is the most evident is the astounding speed of the creature, with some witnesses seeing the creature go an estimated 30 miles an hour in the water. One of the most famous instances of evidence for the Kussie are some pictures taken by an individual named Toshio Komana in 1974. The pictures were taken from a distance, but they depict an unknown animal in the water which appears to have a long neck and a large body. Most Kussie researchers believe it to be a *plesiosaur* of some sort. Since the history of sightings for this creature is fairly recent this arouses suspicions for me. It could be likely that the Kussie is a publicity ploy in order to bring tourists to the lake.

Lake Memphremagog Monster

According to accounts Lake Memphremagog has a beast dwelling in it. Lake Memphremagog is a large lake, on the border between the state of Vermont and Quebec, Canada, which has a surface area of 41 square mile and a depth of 351 feet. Is this lake yet another body of water in Canada which hides a lake monster? For most locals along the lake the answer is 'yes' due to a rich history of stories of a creature in the lake. Nicknamed Memphre by the locals, this creature has been seen for hundreds of years. Even one of the first explorers in America, the Vikings, heard and believed tales of the animal in the lake. The description of the Lake Memphremagog monster is of an elongated, serpentine creature about 30 feet long with a snake-like head, smooth grey skin and sharp teeth. Another description is of a creature that resembles a *plesiosaur* like another nearby cryptid Champ. The Memphremagog Monster has become a local icon because of the sightings and the fame of the animal similar to that of Champ of Lake Champlain and Nessie of Loch Ness. Most scientists believe that Memphre is a simple misidentification of known animals and natural phenomena. While some cryptozoologists think that it could be a relic *plesiosaur* or even a population of giant eels. It is possible that Memphre could have a correlation to other lake monsters seen in Canada. Most Canadian lake monsters are described as eel-like, so this could be evidence for a new species of large eel that lives in the many large lakes of Canada.

Lake Monsters

The name lake monster is one you find everywhere in cryptozoology. Throughout the world there are stories of large unknown aquatic creatures. Most large lakes around the world have, or have had, stories of something mysterious residing in their depths. The descriptions of these creatures vary from a more eel-like animal around 10 to 20 feet long to an animal more akin to a prehistoric *plesiosaur* or *mosasaur*. Lakes that have stories of monsters include Lake Michigan, Lake Okanagan, Lake Tele, Lake Champlain and of course Loch Ness. Yes, it is true that most of these lakes are large and might be able to hold a single unknown animal, but my problem is that each of these lakes would need to hold a sustainable population of large creatures. It is impossible for a single animal to be responsible for the stories for each of the many lake monster stories. Each lake with stories of a lake monster would need to hold a large population of large aquatic animals and still be unrecognized by science. For myself this is improbable; if lake monsters exist there would be hundreds of more sightings. I'm not saying that every lake monster is fictitious or a misidentification of known species, some might be actual unknown species of giant eels and fish, I'm saying that most probably are. Lake monsters are important to cryptozoology because they show how people always love a mystery and might just create one. It is only through thorough investigation can we prove that lake monsters usually live in our heads rather than our lakes

Lake Storsjon Monster

The Lake Storsjon monster is a large lake monster that is seen in the Swedish lake Storsjon. Lake Storsjon has a depth of 300 feet and a surface area of 179.2 miles, making it one of the largest lakes in Sweden. The creature that supposedly dwells in the lake sometimes goes by the name storsjoodjuret which means "great lake monster," this beast has a colorful origin story. The local legend states that once a pair of trolls, Jata and Kata, who lived on the lake were brewing something in their cauldron. A noise came from the cauldron, and a creature with a head of a cat and a serpent's body emerged and then disappeared into the lake. The beast soon grew and was even able to wrap itself around an island in the lake. The legend states that hero Ketil Runske slew the beast in 1635, but there are still sightings of a large anomalous creature in the lake to this day. The modern witnesses describe the creature as a serpentine animal about 20 feet long, with a canine or horse-like head, black colored smooth skin and several humps along its back that are seen in the lake. Even the Swedish government put this creature on the endangered species list but then soon removed it, since its existence was not proven. Most researchers into this creature believe it to be a form of aquatic snake or a giant eel species.

Lake Van Monster

The story of the Lake Van Monster originated in 1995 when several individuals saw a large dark animal in the waters of Lake Van, a lake situated in eastern Turkey with a surface area of 1,450 square miles and a depth of 561 feet. This particular cryptid does not have a cultural history. In the 1990s there were sudden sightings of a creature in the lake. Witnesses state the animal as being about 10 to 20 feet long, with a snake-like head, light-colored skin, an elongated body with four flippers and a humped back. One of the most mysterious pieces of evidence for the Lake Van monster is a video created by a local man which depicts a creature with an elongated head moving across the lake with the body not being able to be seen. Individuals who studied the video soon had their concerns about the authenticity of this evidence. Most researchers who saw the video believe the video is a hoax, as there are no size comparisons in the video and the camera does not pan to the right or left, possibly hiding a boat pulling an object made to resemble a creature. Most researchers into the creature do believe that the creature is a simple hoax, since there is no other evidence. This was probably created to bring tourism to Lake Van and that particular region of Turkey. This instance can show how a simple monster story can bring publicity and intrigue into a region. This particular cryptozoological hoax might have a precedent with many other supposed lake monsters seen across the globe.

Lake Worth Monster

The Lake Worth monster is different from all of the other lake monsters, as this particular creature is not aquatic but a bigfoot-like creature. Lake Worth, small a lake just outside of Fort Worth in north Texas, may harbor a peculiar creature on its shores. The first sightings of this creature occurred 1969, with a local couple reported seeing a large bipedal creature near Lake Worth. The description of this creature is of a humanoid, about 6 to7 feet tall with white fur. Some witnesses state they saw small horns on the creature's head or a more bigfoot-like description. The sightings of the creature were so believed that the local law enforcement and locals created posses to hunt the creature. Most saw nothing except for one incident when the creature threw a tire at the people from a nearby bluff, and then ran off. The locals thought the creature lived on Greer Island, as most of the sightings occurred on this island and that some witnesses claimed that they saw the beast swim to the island. Greer Island is a refuge, so it's possible that a creature was able to survive there, away from the prying eyes of humans. Sightings of the creature ended as soon as it started, causing many left to only wonder what force engulfed Fort Worth. Most later researchers think that the creature was a goatman due to the description, while others think it was a bigfoot with white hair or just simply a hoax. It is possible that this creature was just a white bigfoot that lived for a short time on Greer Island.

Living Dinosaurs

This may sound outrageous but there have been hundreds of documented and historical sightings of what can only be said is a dinosaur. Throughout cultures from all over the world there are oral stories of large reptiles akin to the beasts of the Mesozoic era. These stories include the mokele-mbembe, inkanyamba, irizima, emela-ntouka, nguma monene, mbielu-mbielu-mbielu and muhulu. Most of these stories come from Africa and parts of Asia and South America. It is scientifically improbable that large terrestrial non-avian dinosaurs have survived into the modern day. Some animals from the Mesozoic have survived such as crocodilians, sharks, and birds but dinosaurs are unlikely. Some of these stories might be formed thanks to cultures finding fossils or even misidentification of known animals. It is likely that most of these stories originate in Africa, thanks to the cultural anachronisms of that period. Many descriptions of supposed living dinosaurs don't match what we now know dinosaurs to look like. I'm not saying it's impossible for non-avian dinosaurs to exist in the unexplored regions of the world, but it is very unlikely. These stories were most likely created by individuals to help make the unexplored regions of the world even more fantastical. It is most likely that stories of dinosaurs surviving into recorded history are false but in the natural world there are always possibilities for discoveries that will change the world.

Living Pterosaurs

My views of living pterosaurs are very similar to the ones on living dinosaurs. It is scientifically improbable for *pterosaurs* to still exist today. One of the largest pieces of evidence against living pterosaurs are their descriptions. People report large scale covered bodies with pointed leathery wings, long tails and head crests. This was the view of what pterosaurs looked like in the past but modern paleontology shows that these descriptions are now false. *Pterosaurs* were covered in feather-like filament, had rounded wings, short tails and usually had air sacks in their wings. Descriptions of living *pterosaurs* are anachronistic, an amalgamation of famous *pterosaur* species such as *pteranodon*, a*rdeadactylus* and *quetzalcoatlus*. People at the time described what they thought a *pterosaur* looked like, but later discoveries showed they didn't. I'm suspicious of supposed living *pterosaurs*, due to the lack of actual scientific evidence for them. It is possible that *pterosaur* sightings are misidentifications of known species such as large birds, bats, or even hoaxes. Another explanation is that these eyewitnesses might be seeing an unknown species of bat but even then, the description of a long beak still doesn't make sense. It is highly improbable that pterosaurs survive today but people still say they see them. This might also be due to romanticizing the unknown and how extinct species might still survive today. This can cause people to see an animal that actually isn't there.

Lizard Man

This could be one of the most peculiar humanoid cryptids seen in the Southern U.S. The story of the lizard man started in 1988 when a man named Christopher Davis was driving in Bishopville, South Carolina, where he saw frightening creature. Davis claimed that he saw a bipedal creature with a long tail, scale-covered skin and red eyes run at him from the nearby swamp. Davis got to his vehicle and drove off. This sighting started a large increase of sightings of a reptilian humanoid in Bishopville. The lizard man appears to be a bipedal reptile about 7 feet tall, with red eyes and three toes on both feet. Soon locals believed the creature originated from the nearby Scape Ore Swamp, where most of the sightings occurred. Casts of footprints found near Scape Ore Swamp and believed to belong to this creature show a human-like foot but with three long digits. Local resident's vehicles were being attacked at night by an unknown animal which appeared to be very aggressive. But soon the sightings of the creature stopped, causing many to wonder what exactly this creature was. Later researchers have proven that the supposed lizard man footprints were a hoax and most of the vehicles attacked by this lizard man were actually attacked by local dogs. Due to inconsistencies and lack of evidence most suspect the lizard man to be a simple hoax. This hoax might have been done in order to get publicity for Bishopville, as the sightings renewed tourist interest in the town.

Lobizon

Also spelled lobizone, the lobizon which translates to "son of the wolf." This is yet another unknown werewolf-like canine, but this particular one is seen in South America. The legend of the lobizon originates in Argentina, where most of the sightings of this creature occurs. The legend of the lobizon states that the seventh son of a family will turn into a wolf-like canine during a full moon. This belief is so feared that there have been instances of the seventh son of certain families being abandoned and even being put in asylums due to fear. The canines they turn into are described as being about the size of a wolf with either black or red fur with long ears. Some even claim that the canine can become bipedal demonstrating a possible Bipedal Canine connection to the folklore of the lobizon. Most folklorists and biologists who study the lobizon believe that the creature could be a misidentification of the maned wolf of a feral dog. The story of individuals turning into wolves was most likely a story of a mental illness called lycanthropy that has been passed around orally for generations. Another possible explanation of the lobizon is that it could be a small population of Biped Canines in South America. When the Great American Biotic Interchange happened 3 million years ago the creatures we know as Bipedal Canines were able to travel from their evolutionary origins in North America down to South America via Panama. This isolated population of Bipedal Canines might be the reason for the legend of the lobizon.

Loup-Garou

The loup-garou is an unknown canine seen in the U.S. The sightings of the loup-garou occur in Louisiana's bayous where the Cajuns have a deep fear of this creature. The loup-garou is believed to be is a werewolf-like beast that lives in the desolate bayous of southern Louisiana. One creature that is similar to the loup-garou is the rougarou, another bayou cryptid seen in the same area as the loup-garou. One major factor is that the loup-garou is believed to be more spiritual than the rougarou. The legend of the loup-garou originated in France where the creature was known as "loup-garoux" meaning werewolf. This folklore soon came to Louisiana where most of the French settlers migrated, and the creature became the loup-garou. The Cajuns describe the loup-garou as a wolf-like canine with long grey to black fur, biped, with a humanoid shape and canine head. Most folklorists think that the loup-garou is a simple legend that was moved to Louisiana via the French settlers. One possibility is that the French did bring stories of the loup-garou but there was already an existing bipedal canine creature in Louisiana which became the story of the rougarou. Another possibility is that the loup-garou is a kind of spiritual being or just another name for the rougarou. Since the Cajuns put more spiritual attributes to the rougarou, the legend of the loup-garou was born as a more spiritual or demonic-like being.

Loveland Frog

This humanoid cryptid was first seen in Loveland, Ohio, in the 1950s. The story goes that a local man was driving along a road just outside of Loveland near the Little Miami River. He saw three figures just off the road and thought they were humans until he could see that the creatures were anything but. He described the creature as about 3 to 4 feet tall with humanoid bodies, a frog-like face, green skin and heads with large mouths. One of the most peculiar aspects to the incident is that one of the creatures was holding a device that the witness described as similar to a wand that shot out sparks. Soon after the sighting it was forgotten until a similar incident occurred in 1972. In this incident a police officer named Ray Shockey was driving in Loveland when he saw creatures very similar to those seen in the 1950s. This soon made many individuals think that these creatures were back from wherever they came from. Soon afterwards, the sightings stopped as soon as they started. Many have their own theories of what the creatures were. One theory is that they are unknown aquatic creatures, as the sightings occurred near the Little Miami River, it is possible that the creatures live in the river. Another possible explanation is misidentification of a known species, or a hoax done by a yet unknown party. Due to a lack of recent sightings, it is likely that the Loveland frogs were nothing but overactive imaginations and mass hysteria.

Mahamba

If the supposed relic dinosaurs, relic pterosaurs and giant turtles weren't enough, the Congo supposedly also is home to a gigantic unknown crocodile. The indigenous Congolese people call this creature the mahamba, and say that it lives in and around Lake Likouala. The description of the mahamba is of a colossal crocodilian, about 50 feet long with a massive head and long tail. One of the first westerners to confirm these tales was Belgian explorer John Rinehart Warner in the 1890s. He had two personal encounters with crocodiles over 40 feet long. This counters the idea that the largest crocodile in Africa is the Nile crocodile, which reaches lengths about 16 feet long. These measures are truly diminutive when compared to the mahamba. The largest known extant crocodilian species is the Indonesian crocodile which reaches lengths about 20 feet long. The problem is that the Indonesian crocodile is not even indigenous to Africa. Some of the ideas of the origin of the mahamba is that it is a relic population of prehistoric giant crocodiles. One candidate could be *dienosuchus* which lived 65 million years ago and reached about 35 feet long. Another major likelihood could be *sarosuchus* which lived 112 million years ago and reached 40 feet long and was found in Africa where the mahamba is seen today. It could also be that the mamlambo is a known species of crocodile, but due to its environment, has the ability to grow into measures not yet seen in their species.

Maine Mutant

The Maine mutant is a canine cryptid seen primarily in Maine and the northeast U.S. The story of the Maine mutant started in the early 2000s when locals in Maine heard of an unknown creature, stalking in their local woods and fields. The witnesses claimed they heard peculiar growls and howls at night which they could not contribute to any known canines in the United States. Along with the strange noises of the creature attacks that were blamed for the animal, the victims of the animal were livestock but also a high frequency of attacks on domestic dogs blamed on this creature. The description of the creature was of a canine about two feet tall at the shoulder, a long bushy tail, large eyes, black fur, a sloped back similar to a hyena, long tufted ears, a short muzzle and long legs. The individuals in the area believed that the creature was a feral dog or even a wolf. The attacks stopped as soon as a body was discovered in the town of Turner, Maine. The creature soon named the Turner beast was believed to be the creature perpetrating these attacks. Soon DNA testing was performed, which revealed the creature was a hybrid of domestic dog and wolf. Which leaves people to wonder if there are more of these creatures out there, in the wilds of the United States. Others suspect that the Turner beast isn't the Maine mutant, and that this creature is another cryptid known as the shunka warakin. The shunka warakin has a very similar description to the Maine mutant and the name even translates to "carrying off dogs."

Mamlambo

The mamlambo is a lake monster seen in South Africa. The sightings of the mamlambo occur along the Mzintlava River where the indigenous culture of the Zulu people have a deep cultural history of this beast. The Zulu legends state that the mamlambo is a giant beast that dwells in the river and will emerge from the water in order to consume its prey – either livestock or tribesmen. Some stories of the mamlambo say that the creature is more akin to a river deity. The descriptions of the mamlambo are diverse, from a giant fish about 6 to 9 feet long, to a reptilian serpentine creature about 60 feet long with a horse-like head, green scale-covered skin and four short legs. The Zulu people believe that individuals that go missing or are killed in the Mzintlava River are likely due to the mamlambo. There are not many sightings of the mamlambo today but one of the most recent incidents with the mamlambo is when several local individuals were killed in the river and locals blamed the deaths on this creature. The local authorities disagreed and said that the deaths were due to flooding in the river. The most prevailing theory of what the mamlambo is is a surviving dinosaur or even a giant indigenous fish species. It is likely the mamlambo is a yet to be discovered species of large fish that dwells in the Mzintlava River.

Mande-barung

The mande-barung is a large unknown hominid seen in northern India. Most of the sightings of the mande-barung occur in the Garo Hills of northern India and Bangladesh where there isn't a large population of people and enough forest to hide a large bipedal primate. Mande-barung, which means "wild people" in the indigenous dialect, have been in the legends of the Indian people for centuries and are seen as just a part of the natural world. The description of the mande-barung is of a bipedal primate about 5 to 7 feet tall, red to black fur that covers the body, long arms, human-like face, similar to the description of other cryptid primates seen in Southern Asia. Many call the mande-barung the "low land Yeti" due to the similarities of the yeti and the mande-barung in their physical description and behavior. Most cryptozoologists believe that the mande-barung is related to the other cryptid primates seen in Asia like the Bukit Timor monkey man, yeti, yeren, nguoi-rung and batutut. Some of these animals may even come from the same species of origin. Researchers believe that the mande-barung is a living relative of *gigantopithecus* that has been able to get smaller in order to hide more effectively in our modern world. Others suspect this creature is yet another example for a surviving species of hominid like *homo-erectus* of *homo-habilis*.

Mangarisaoka

The mangarisaoka is a cryptid seen in Madagascar. Unlike any of the other cryptids written in this book, the mangarisaoka is not a primate, aquatic animal, canine, feline or a flying animal but an unknown ungulate. The indigenous peoples of northern Madagascar believe that the mangarisaoka is an equine living in the high and treacherous alpine regions of Madagascar. The mangarisaoka is supposed to resemble a donkey with long floppy ears that can cover the face, which is how the creature got its name which means "whose ears that cover the chin." The mangarisaoka is around 4 feet tall at the shoulder with short brown fur, with long horse-like legs and a donkey-like head. The mangarisaoka is one particular cryptid that is not well known, and many don't even know about. One of the first western cryptozoologists to study and write about the mangarisaoka was Bernard Huevelmans in has 1955 book *On The Track Of Unknown Animals*. Huevekmans describe the creature as "a donkey with floppy ears, round horse-like hooves,with grey or brown fur, brays like a donkey and lives in the highlands of Madagascar." Most do think that the mangarisaoka is an unknown equine species that dwells in remote regions of Madagascar. Due to the fact that there aren't any sightings of this creature today it is likely that this ungulate is already extinct. We can only hope this creature has been able to survive in the mountains of Madagascar and still lives there till this day.

Mapinguari

The mapinguari is a large unknown creature seen in South America. The indigenous peoples of Brazil, especially in and near the Amazon, have told tales of a large dangerous animal that could kill very easily and should be feared by any who meet it. One of the first ways that the mapinguari was said to look like was a creature with one eye, about 9 feet tall with red fur and a large mouth in its stomach that emitted a foul odor, and which had a bad attitude towards humans and their animals. Soon after that Western cryptozoologist went to South America and studied the mapinguari for themselves and came to another conclusion. What most researchers thought was that the mapinguari was a bigfoot-like creature which lived in the jungles. Soon after that an ornithologist named David Oren developed a theory that the mapinguari isn't a primate but an extinct ground sloth that once lived in Pleistocene-era South America. This was based on a description of a herbivorous creature that is quadrupedal but can go on two with red fur, long claws, a sloth-like head, and a horrid odor. This soon created the idea that the mapinguari could be an extinct ground sloth called a *mylodon* which once lived in the regions where the mapinguari is seen today. It is possible that the *mylodon* was able to survive the late Quaternary mass-extinction and has adapted to a life living in the thick jungles of the Amazon. Even Karl Shuker stated that a medium-size ground sloth would be a good identity for the enigmatic mapinguari.

Marked Hominids

Marked Hominids are a variant of unknown primate seen across the higher latitudes of the Northern Hemisphere. Marked Hominids are seen primarily in colder climates in remote regions of Asia and North America especially in Siberia and Northern Canada. The cryptozoologist Loren Coleman and Patrick Huyghe came up with the term "Marked Hominids" to describe a particular type of unknown hominids seen across the world. The description of Marked Hominids are similar to the description of other unknown primates but with distinguishing features. The description of Marked Hominids are of a bipedal primate about 6 to 8 feet tall with wide shoulders, human-like faces with no visible neck and dark colored fur. The only real difference for Marked Hominids and other cryptid primates is that they have patches of white to lighter colored fur on the limbs and head, similar to some known primates that use this fur for courtship. Another aspect is that Marked Hominids are seen as more human-like, similar to the almas of Russia and even appear to have a primitive culture and dialect. Due to this many believe that these creatures may be a different species from the other cryptid primates seen in the same regions. A possible candidate for these creatures are Neandertals or Denisovans which both morphologically and genetically are very similar to humans. It is also possible that Marked Hominids are creatures such as sasquatch and the almas but have a genetic mutation that causes these light patches of hair.

Marozi

The marozi is a large cryptid feline seen in Africa, primarily in mountainous regions of Eastern Africa, especially in the Aberdares Mountains in Kenya. The marozi is very similar to the African lion except it has a darker colored spotted coat. The indigenous cultures of the region have an oral tradition of these "spotted lions" and their belief is that they originated from a hybridization of a leopard and lion. Soon after Westerners came to Africa, they reported seeing spotted lions and believed these animals to be the marozi from native legends. The description of the marozi is of a feline with the body shape of a lion, smaller than a lion but larger than a leopard, with a tan-colored coat with darker tan-colored spots on top. Many believe that the marozi is simply a juvenile lion, as lions when young do have a spotted coat. Later researchers like Karl Shuker and Bernard Heuvelmans believe that the marozi could be a subspecies of lion, as the marozi have different behavioral and morphological traits than the regular African lion. The marozi is seen to be solitary rather than in a pride, like the regular African lion. It could be possible that the marozi is a population of lions which have adapted to a solitary alpine environment. The answers to what the marozi are might never be answered, as there haven't been any marozi sightings since the 1930s. This has caused many to suspect the marozi has already become extinct.

Mbielu-Mbielu-Mbielu

The mbielu-mbielu-mbielu is a large unknown semi aquatic animal seen in Africa. The Likouala Lake and swamp region of the Congo have a history of sightings of unknown animals, but this could be one of the most peculiar of these creatures. Translated to "the animal with plates growing out of its back," the mbielu-mbielu-mbielu has been a part of the indigenous peoples of the Congo folklore and legends for a long time. The name for the creature is based on the description of the creature. The creature is always seen in the water with its back protruding out, similar to crocodile. The creature is about 20 feet long, with a large body with plates running down its back similar to the prehistoric *stegosaurus* of the Jurassic Era, a small reptilian head and green scaled skin. The natives do not know if the creature has legs or fins, as it is only seen in an aquatic environment. One of the first cryptozoologists to study the creature was Roy Mackal, who came up with the idea that the mbielu-mbielu-mbielu is a relic species of *stegosaurus*. Due to the similarity between the description and geographic proximity of the mbielu-mbielu-mbielu and another cryptid, the nguma-monene, I suspect that both are in fact the same creature. The mbielu-mbielu-mbielu is most likely not a dinosaur but a misidentification of crocodiles. It is also possible that it is a new species of monitor lizard like what the nguma-monene is suspected to be.

Megalania

When the Aborigines first came to Australia, they told legends of a giant 20-foot-long lizard that was not to be taken lightly. Soon paleontologists discovered a reptile which matches that exact description: megalania which means "ancient giant butcher." Megalania was the largest reptile on Earth since the dinosaurs; most estimate it being between 20 and 25 feet long. It preyed on the plethora of megafauna found in Australia at the time. Most scientists think that megalania went extinct about 50,000 years ago at the late Pleistocene epoch, which means that the Aborigines and megalania had to have interacted in the past. Recently some individuals in Australia have questioned if it really did go extinct. In modern-day Australia there have been sightings of a creature whose description matches exactly to megalania. Even early settlers into Australia saw large lizards they estimated were about 20 to 30 feet long and roamed the wilds of the outback. Today there have been sightings of megalanias in the same forests and deserts that they roamed in prehistory. There have even been giant lizard-like footprints found in the Australian outback which belong to a lizard five times the largest extant lizard in Australia, the perentie. One of Australia's most well-known cryptozoologists, Rex Gilroy has put years of research into the megalania and believes that the Aborigines still see the megalania till this day. Most think that megalania could not possibly exist today due to their sheer size, but in the land down under you never know what to expect.

Megalodon

Megalodon is the largest shark that has ever lived. Megalodon was a shark that many think could have reached lengths of 60 feet long, megalodon lived about 23 to 2.5 million years ago. Most paleontologists believe that megalodon went extinct about 2.5 million years ago due to climate change. This is not that long ago, when compared to the history of life on Earth. Some modern sightings have forced some to wonder if megalodon really did go extinct. Today there have been a myriad of sightings of sharks that match the description of megalodon all across the globe. Most sightings occur along the Equator and supposedly on whale migratory routes. Which would make since due to that megalodon predated whales when they in their heyday. One possible evidence for the survival of megalodon were two megalodon teeth brought up by the *HMS Challenger* in 1875. The teeth were only about 10,000 years old, long after the period that mainstream science states megalodon went extinct. The sightings of megalodon occur all over the warmer parts of the world but one of the most known supposed megalodons is the "Diablo negro" which means "black devil" of the Sea of Cortez off the coast of Mexico. Most do think that this creature could be a megalodon. It is possible that megalodon has survived into our recent times but due to the changes in our oceans caused by climate change and man, it is likely that megalodon is already extinct.

Mermaids

One of the most well-known creatures that is unknown to science are mermaids. From Japan to Greece there are sightings and a deep folklore of aquatic beings which are a mix between humans and fish. Most maritime cultures and people have tales or folklore regarding mermaids or merfolk that inhabit their local bodies of water, especially in seas and oceans. Even though there are a plethora of locations of mermaid folklore, description of these creatures are almost all very similar. They describe a creature which is aquatic with the torso of a human and with the bottom half of a fish. Most mainstream scientists think that these are just simple fictional legends and misidentification of known marine life, certainly pinnipeds and manatees. Mostly due to the sheer number of different cultures and the geographic distance from one another with very similar legends one has to wonder if these cultures are describing a real creature. One possible explanation is the Aquatic Ape Theory that states that at one point homo-sapiens were adapting to a marine lifestyle, but this theory has been disproven thanks to anatomists and anthropologists. Another explanation could be a misidentification of known animals like dugongs and manatees, which throughout history have been shown to be animals that have been mistaken as mermaids. It is unlikely that an aquatic culture similar to ours ever existed, but this question helps show how an unbelievable tale can still bring interest to a rarely explored subject like cryptozoology.

Michigan Dogman

The Michigan dogman is another instance of a bipedal canine that is seen in the Midwest of the United States. The Michigan dogman is seen in several locations all over Michigan, but most occur in the northwest region of the state. This region has a history of sightings of a creature that can be closely described as a werewolf. Most anecdotal accounts state that the story of the Michigan dogman originated in 1887 when locals in Wexford County saw a peculiar bipedal creature with a canine-like head and humanoid body. This matches with the modern-day sightings of the dogman. The description of the Michigan dogman is of a canine about 7 feet tall, with a large body, a bushy tail, brown to black fur, canine-like legs and either a wolf-like head or a more pitbull-like head; this is way to differentiate this creature from most bipedal canines. Similar to most other bipedal canines the Michigan dogman is seen primarily while crossing roads or on the side of roads. One interesting part of the dogman and other bipedal canines is that they are seen near crossroads, churches, and even graveyards. The reason for this is unknown. One characteristic that is different with this creature from most other bipedal canines is the belief that it is more spiritual in nature. This belief might form thanks to the legends of werewolves and shapeshifters being prevalent in Native American mythology. The Michigan dogman isn't different from other bipedal canines, the only difference is the name where it is reported to have been seen.

Minhocao

The minhocao is a very peculiar cryptid that is seen in South America. The name minhocao means "giant earthworm" in the local dialect. The name implies that the minhocao is a giant subterranean animal similar to a massive worm like the creatures from the movie series *Tremors*. The story originates in the mid-1800s when locals in Brazil found strange burrows and unearthed soil around their properties. One of the most famous incidents in the history of the minhacoa is in Brazil in 1849 when a local man named Joao de Deos found a large amount of unearthed soil on his property, presumably from a minhacao. The usual description of the minhocao is of an animal about 4 to 5 feet long with armor-plating on the outside of the animal and either a serpentine body or a body more that of an armadillo. Another famous sighting occurred in the 1890s when a man saw a minhocao on land and he stated it appeared to be an armadillo about 3 feet tall and 5 feet long and with a pig-like snout. This has caused a debate over what the minhocao is. The cryptozoologist Karl Shuker thinks that the creature is a giant *caecilian*. While Bernard Huevelmans thinks that it is an extinct species named a *glyptodont* which once lived in Pleistocene era South America. The *glyptodont* looked very similar to extant armadillos but were the size of a large pig. Most paleontologists think the *glyptodont* went extinct during the late Pleistocene but it's possible that small populations have survived into the recent past.

Ryan Edwards

Mitla

The mitla is either an unknown canine-like felid or feline-like canid. First written about by the explorer Lieutenant Colonel Percy Fawcett in the early 1900s while in Bolivia, Fawcett described the mitla as a "black dog-like cat about the size of a foxhound" whice lived in the Rio Madeira region of Bolivia. Percy Fawcett stated that he personally had 2 brief sightings of the mitla but was never able to get a deeper description of the creature or any physical evidence. Even though Fawcett stated that the indigenous population had the stories of the ferocity of the mitla, he never witnessed any attacks for himself. After Fawcett there were many individuals that tried to find the mitla including Jersey Zoo director Jeremy Mallinson in 1962 and Roy Mackal and Karl Shuker hunted the mitla while in Bolivia. Even Ivan T. Sanderson on a trip to Bolivia tried to hunt the mitla but all that tried weren't able to come to a solid conclusion of what the mitla truly is. There are many theories of what the mitla is. Roy Mackal believed that the mitla was a melanistic bush dog or even an undiscovered subspecies of the same animal. Karl Shuker thinks that the mitla could be an unknown canine rather than a feline. Shuker believes that the short-eared dog, a canine indigenous to South America, is a likely candidate for the mitla.

114

Mngwa

The mngwa, also called nunda, is a cryptid feline that is seen in the African country of Tanzania. The mngwa originates from the indigenous people of Tanzania who created the name mngwa which translates to "the strange one." The natives have been telling stories of the mngwa for centuries and have a deep fear of this creature. The mngwa is different from all other felines in Africa, due to the size and physical description. The description of the mngwa is of a feline about the size of a donkey (larger than a lion), dark grey fur, lighter colored stripes with a long tail, large head, and long tail. The mngwa also cannot roar but purrs like a domestic cat. The mngwa is nocturnal, which matches with most large felines found in Africa. Later Europeans started to see this creature and stated that the mngwa is different from all other felines found in Tanzania. There have been many theories of what the mngwa is. Bernard Heuvelmans believed that the mngwa is a giant species of the golden cat, but the golden cat measures only 4 to 5 feet long; very small when compared to the mngwa. Another possibility for the mngwa is that because it can't roar, it is a relative to the cheetah. The felinae, the smaller cats can't roar either, so it's possible the mngwa belongs to this group of felines. It might possibly be a basal form of cheetah which has found an environmental niche similar to the tiger of India, a solitary nocturnal hunter. This might even explain the striped coat due to it being an example of convergent evolution with the tiger's coat.

Moa

The moa was a giant terrestrial bird native to New Zealand in the Pleistocene epoch. The moa had 9 different species which varied in size from 12 feet tall to only 4 feet tall. The moa flourished in New Zealand until most believe it was over hunted by the indigenous Maori people. Most believe the moa went extinct about 1300 C.E. Or did they? Locals in New Zealand have to ask themselves if the moa really go extinct. Individuals today see a bird that matches exactly to the description of the "extinct" moa. They describe a bird with brown feathers, about 5 to 7 feet tall with a long neck, a large body, a small head and no visible tail. The belief in living moas originated in the 17th century when sailors went to New Zealand and saw large birds that looked very similar to the moa. In modern day New Zealand there have been many expeditions to find the moa. One cryptozoologist who has started expeditions to New Zealand and studied the moa is Australian Rex Gilroy. Most researchers into the moa believe that the smaller species of the moa could have the ability to survive in the lush jungles of New Zealand, especially in the alpine regions of the island. So the moa might be yet another example of a Lazarus taxon.

Mokele-mbembe

The mokele-mbembe could be one of the most well-known African cryptids in cryptozoology. Mokele-mbembe which translates to "the one that stops the flow of rivers" in the Lingala language, is a large reptilian cryptid seen in the Congo, especially near Lake Tele. The indigenous population have been telling legends of the mokele-mbembe for centuries and have a deep respect for it. The natives describe the mokele-mbembe as a creature that is the size of an elephant with a long serpentine tail, a long neck, and a small head, with four thick legs, and thick grey to brown colored skin. The mokele-mbembe is seen primarily in the water, but there have been sightings of the creature on land. One of the first cryptozoologists who heard about the mokele-mbembe was Roy Mackal who suspects the mokele-mbembe to be a species of *sauropod* dinosaur. These animals were supposed to go extinct 65 million years ago. The evidence is that the natives would draw out a picture of a mokele-mbembe, it matched exactly to a Mesozoic *sauropod*. The likelihood for a surviving *sauropod* is very low. Is it possible that this creature has been misconstrued in order to make the idea of living dinosaurs and Africa as a prehistoric primordial continent. It is more likely that the mokele-mbembe is a cultural memory of known animals that once inhabited the Congo basin such as giraffes and rhinos. The idea that a population of *sauropods* survive in the jungles of the Congo even though it would be amazing if true, is most likely not.

Momo

Momo is a regional name for a bigfoot-like creature seen in Louisiana, Missouri, in the 1970s. Momo, short for Missouri monster, is a peculiar bipedal primate that appeared in Louisiana. suddenly and violently. The incident started in 1971 when several local teenagers saw a strange humanoid figure in the local woods and bottomlands. The description of the creature is of a creature about 7 feet tall with long black fur covering the face, long arms, very similar to the bigfoot seen in the Pacific Northwest. One thing that differentiated the Momo from some of the other bigfoot-like cryptids is that the Momo is described to be more violent, some witnesses stating that they saw the creature with blood on its fur and even carrying dead animals. In the area of Momo sightings there was also a period of animal disappearance, especially dogs. Heightened aggression is a characteristic found in the bigfoot and bigfoot-like creatures seen in the American south. The sightings only lasted about 2 weeks, leaving the area puzzled. All that was left were a couple of tridactyl, or three toed footprints. The footprints were analyzed and were shown to be from a primate – most peculiar because there isn't any known primate with only three digits. It is possible that Momo was just a genetically mutated bigfoot or Nape that found itself on the outskirts of a small Missouri town in the 1970s.

Mongolian Death Worm

The Mongolian death worm is another cryptid that sounds unbelievable, but it is still seen by many individuals and has a strong belief system behind it. The Mongolian death worm is seen in the Gobi Desert of Mongolia where the first witnesses to the creature were the indigenous nomadic people of the Gobi. The local name for the creature is "allghoi-khorkhoi" which means "intestine worm" because of the color and appearance of the creature. The local cultures describe the creature as about 4 to 10 feet long with red skin, a large hideous head, the creature supposedly spits acid at its prey and is also able to create an electric charge in order to kill prey. The Mongolian death worm is also stated to be subterranean; this is the reason for its elusiveness. Some of the first westerners to study the death worm were Soviet scientists from the USSR. One of the first written descriptions of the creature was the 1926 book by Roy Chapman Andrews *On the Trail of Ancient Man*. After the USSR's research many more scientists and cryptozoologists have tried discovering this peculiar creature. One of the most prolific researchers into the creature is Ivan Mackerle, who has done many expeditions to find the creature in the 1990s. The expeditions to discover the death worm are unsuccessful at finding evidence for it. Most think that this creature could be an unknown species of reptile, like a snake or limbless lizard. Others believe it to be a giant undiscovered worm species.

Monkey Man of England

Also known as the wuduwasa and Green Man, this is a name used for unknown primates that are seen throughout the U.K. From Scotland, Ireland, Britain, and Wales there are sightings of large bipedal primates reminiscent of a bigfoot seen in the U.S. Since the medieval age there has existed a body of folklore concerning large human-like beings covered with fur and living the woods. Some of the first names for these creatures were the Green Men, as they were believed to be forest beings; the name Green Man demonstrates that belief. Another name was wuduwasa, the name used for the bigfoot-like creatures seen in Britain. The common description for these creatures is a bipedal primate creature about 6 to 8 feet tall with black to brown fur which covers that body and very human-like face and proportions. These cryptids do not get as much news as the American bigfoot and other unknown primates, yet there is still a community that is dedicated to finding these creatures, individuals include Nick Redfern, Anna Nekaris, and Adam Davies. One possible explanation for these creatures is that they are surviving Neanderthals which crossed over a land bridge known as Doggerland during the Pleistocene era and still live in the U.K today. Another slightly more likely explanation is the misidentification of escaped simian exotic pets. I find it unlikely a creature as large as sasquatch can persist in Britain.

Mono-Grande

The mono-grande, Spanish for "large monkey" is a bigfoot-like creature seen throughout Central and South America. The mono-grande obtained its name as the individuals who saw this creature described it as having the appearance of a large monkey or ape. The first people to encounter the mono-grande were the indigenous Indian tribes of Central America and Northern South America. Sightings of the mono-grande range from northern Mexico to as far south as Brazil. The description of the mono-grande is of a very muscular primate about 5 to 7 feet tall with black to red fur which covers the body, a human-like face, and large feet. Later explorers like the Spanish encountered the mono-grande also, and even stated that the mono-grande were more human-like, claiming that they live in huts and primitive villages. One of the most famous incidents of the mono-grande occurred in 1920 when the explorer Francois de Loys shot a large unknown creature, soon named the "De Loys Ape." This creature was photographed and thought to be as large as a human. Many later cryptozoologists have come to the conclusion that the picture is a hoax, and is merely a spider monkey made to look larger than it really is. One possible explanation for the mono-grande is that it is a large unknown monkey in Central America. Another is that it's a population of bigfoot that have adapted to the tropical jungles of Central America.

Morag

Morag is yet another large aquatic lake monster seen in Loch Morar, in Scotland, only about 10 miles from the famous Loch Ness. Loch Morar has a total surface area of 10 square miles and a depth of about 1,000 feet. This is a lake that could hide a large creature. Morag is the local name used for the creature. The first sightings of Morag supposedly date back to 1887, when locals first started to see a strange shape in the waters of Morar. The description of Morag is very similar to other lake monsters, certainly Nessie; a creature from 8 to 40 feet long with a long neck, 1 to 4 humps that are seen in the water, a horse-like head, skin dark in color, and four flippers. Most sightings occur when witnesses see a long neck protrude out of the water with a small head at the end, or a large wake in the water supposedly caused by the creature's humps. Some of the best evidence for Morag were 2 photographs taken in 1977. The pictures show a strange shape in the loch with humps that are several feet from each other. Most who study the pictures believe they are genuine. The researchers into Morag think, because of the similarities of the description and the vicinity of the two lochs, that Morag and Nessie could be the same creature or related. Another possibility is that due to the fairly recent history of Morag, it might be a publicity stunt to bring tourists from Loch Ness to Loch Morar.

Mothman

This aerial cryptid was first seen in Point Pleasant, West Virginia in 1966. The story of the Mothman starts with local teens from Point Pleasant going to a local hangout called the TNT Area, an abandoned World War II-era munitions factory. Most of the first witnesses described a fiendish figure, describing it as a creature about 6 to 7 feet tall with a humanoid body, large leathery wings about 10 to 12 feet wide. and glowing red eyes. The local individuals soon named the creature "Mothman" from its' appearance and large wings. Sightings of the Mothman was just one of a series of abnormal phenomena in Point Pleasant. Residents in Point Pleasant reported strange phone calls at night from an unknown individual, residents also heard footsteps on roofs. Other residents reported their T.V sets showing strange shapes and even being warned of a disaster. This all culminated 1967 with the collapse of the Silver Bridge that spanned the Ohio River. Most witnesses saw a strange figure on the bridge which they believed was the Mothman. Later individuals suspected that Mothman was warning people about the devastating collapse, or even caused it. Most researchers think that Mothman could be an alien or even a being from another plane of existence. Other researchers suspect the misidentification of known species such as owls might be the real identity of the Mothman.

Muhalu

The muhalu, a large aggressive ape is believed to be a hominid-like primate that inhabits the desolate forests of the Democratic Republic of the Congo. The first individuals to encounter the muhalu are the indigenous tribes of the region, who tell tales of the ferocity and violence of the muhalu. The natives believe that this ape utilizes trees to sleep in but spends the day on the ground. The description of the muhalu is of a bipedal primate about 6 to 8 feet tall, with long black fur except for the face, which has lighter colored fur, human-like feet and is otherwise similar to other cryptid primates seen throughout the world. One of the first Westerners to research and look for the muhalu was Italian explorer Attilio Gatti, who talked to the natives, who told him that the muhalu lived in the Ituri Forest of the Democratic Republic of the Congo. Soon after cryptozoologist Ivan T. Sanderson pursued this cryptid, believing it was related to other cryptid primates seen in Africa. The most prolific theory for the identity of this creature is that it is a surviving hominid, possibly *homo-erectus* or even a species of *australopithecus* or *paranthropus* which both do match the description quite well. Even the behavior of sleeping in trees then walking on the ground is believed to be a trait of early hominid species.

Muhuru

The muhuru is supposed to be a surviving dinosaur seen in the African country of Kenya. The first documented account of the muhuru occurred in 1963 when missionary Cal Bombay and his wife were driving along the Rift Valley. They were abruptly stopped by an unexpected hazard in the road, a large lizard with armored skin, about 9 to 12 feet long with dark grey skin, plate-like protrusions out of the creature's back, a lizard-like head, a clubbed tail and four large thick legs. The sighting was not well known until in 1998 when Karl Shuker published the report and even interviewed Bombay and believed his account. Another cryptozoologist who took time to pursue the muhuru is William Gibbons who thought it could be a surviving dinosaur. One possible connection to the muhuru is the mbielu-mbielu-mbielu of the Congo which description is similar to the muhuru. Most researchers think that the muhuru could possibly be a surviving *stegosaur* which has been able to survive in Africa. One thing that does not match with *stegosaurus* is that they are not believed to have clubbed tails. This matches more directly to *Ankylosaurs* that do have armored skin similar to the muhuru. These discrepancies might show possible falsities in the story. I have shown in the past how I'm not the biggest proponent for surviving dinosaurs and I hold the muhuru in the same light. It is possible that the story of the muhuru is just an exaggeration of a known lizard or a planned hoax done because of a misconception of African fauna.

Nahuelito

The nahuelito is a lake monster observed in Lake Nahuel Huapi in Northern Patagonia and Argentina. Lake Nahuel Huapi has a surface area of 205 square miles and a depth of 1,440 feet. It's a very large lake with a stable food source of trout and other fish species for a large animal. Starting with the lore of the indigenous people, the Mapuche, which tell tales of a giant aquatic saurian living in the lake. The description of the nahuelito is of a plesiosaur-like creature with the neck similar to a swan, a large body with a small head, humps on the back and dark colored skin. The nahuelito wasn't really studied until the 1920s, when there was a rash of sightings of the creature. There were even several photographs that supposedly depict the creature. Many considered the nahuelito as South America's own Nessie and was soon pursued, as avidly as Nessie of Scotland. Nahuelito has become a cryptozoological celebrity in Argentina. One interesting aspect is that the cuero, another aquatic cryptid from South America, is also believed to dwell in the lake. There have also been sightings of supposed living *pterosaurs* on the cliffs and mountains near Nahuel Huapi. This can cause one to question the existence of this creature. It is possible that there is a biological animal behind these sightings, but due to the celebrity of this creature and the overall influx of tourism because of the nahuelito, it is hard to tell the truth from reality.

Nandi-bear

The Nandi-bear is a large dangerous mammal seen in Eastern Africa. The name derives from the Nandi People of Kenya who were the first people to encounter the nandi-bear. The "bear" part of the Nandi-bear is due to the size and description of the creature. The description of the Nandi-bear is of a creature 5 feet tall at the shoulder, a sloped back with a large head, spotted coat with long legs, and a small tail similar to a bear. The Nandi people state that the Nandi-bear has a peculiar eating habit, supposedly feeding on the brains of humans first, and then eating the rest of the body. In modern days there have been a number of sightings of the Nandi-bear, especially on Nandi Tribes land. There have been many hypotheses put forward to explain what the Nandi-bear is. Karl Shuker thought that the creature could be a surviving remnant of extinct giant hyenas that once roamed most of Africa in prehistory. Others think that the creature could be a species of bear which has managed to survive in Africa. One of the most recent theories put forward is that the Nandi-bear isa species of giant extinct baboon called *dinopithecus*. This was a baboon about the size of a black bear that was found in Africa. Thanks to the size and stature of *dinopithecus* a person might think this primate is actually a large bear. Also due to the aggressiveness of modern baboons it's believed that the *dinopithecus* might have had a very similar disposition. This might cause the stories of the Nandi-bear being dangerous towards humans.

Napes

The name napes was coined by the famous cryptozoologist Loren Coleman in the 1960s. The name is short for North American Ape. These creatures are very different from other cryptid primates seen in North America. The description of napes is of a chimp-like creature with long black fur, quadrupedal, but can do bipedal locomotion for a short period of time. One distinctive feature for Napes is that they have a divergent big toe like chimpanzees and gorillas, demonstrating an arboreal lifestyle. Loren Coleman was one of the first to find evidence for these creatures in 1962 when he found footprints in Decatur, Illinois. Napes are more anthropoid than the humanoid bigfoots that are seen in the U.S. These creatures inhabit the swamp and bottomlands of the Southeast and the Midwest primarily along the Mississippi river. Creatures such as the Fouke Monster and Momo are believed to be napes and different from the sasquatch of the Pacific Northwest. Napes are more violent than bigfoots and can swim, a characteristic not found in most great apes. Loren Coleman believes that napes are the surviving population of a prehistoric ape species named *dryopithecus*. *Dryopithecus* was indigenous to Asia, Africa, and Europe in the Pleistocene epoch. *Dryopithecus* appeared to be evolving to be more human-like which might explain why modern napes are seen walking bipedally at times. It is possible that relic populations of *dryopithecus* still live today in the swamps of the U.S.

Ndendeki

The ndendeki is a species of giant turtle seen in the Congo. This reptilian rascal is seen primarily in the swamps and rivers near Lake Tele and the Likouala-aux-Herbes River. This region is famous for several other cryptids that are seen in the same area. The indigenous people of the Congo were the first to tell tales of the ndendeki, which they claim to be quite different from the other dinosaur-like cryptids seen in the area. The description of the ndendeki is of a giant semi-aquatic turtle, about 13 feet in diameter and with green skin and shell. This exceeds the largest indigenous turtle to Africa, the soft-shell turtle which doesn't exceed about 3 feet in diameter. The largest known turtle is the leatherback sea turtle which reaches 7 to 10 feet in length, still small when compared to the size the ndendeki supposedly reaches. But there is still one possible candidate for the ndendeki, the *archelon*, a giant marine turtle from the Cretaceous era. The *archelon* reached lengths of 13 feet long and were indigenous to North America. This has led some to theorize that the *archelon* could still be alive in the jungles of the Congo. This particular hypothesis isn't very likely, as the *archelon* was a marine turtle that was fully aquatic. There are several other theories that might explain the ndendeki. Roy Mackal believes the ndendeki could be an entirely new species of turtle not yet discovered by science; other researchers suspect that the ndendeki could be a gigantic example of a known species of turtle.

Nessie

Possibly one of the most famous cryptids in the world, Nessie is a well-known lake monster. Seen in the Scottish Loch Ness, this cryptid is similar to many other aquatic cryptids seen throughout the world. Nessie came to the attention of the world in 1933, thanks to a series of sightings documented in the local newspapers. The "Surgeon's Photograph" taken in 1934 showed a creature in the lake. Later it was shown that the picture was a hoax. The description of Nessie is of a creature about 10 to 20 feet long with a large body, long neck that ends with a small head, four flippers and a tail with darker colored skin. Even though the creature has been in the public eye since the 1930s there is a rich history of peculiar aquatic creatures in Loch Ness. In 565 A.D a man named Saint Columba supposedly cast out a water creature from the River Ness which flows into the loch. The Loch Ness monster is now a household name, thanks to a series of researchers into the creature and several videos and pictures that supposedly depict the animal. One of the most well-known researchers is Adrian Shine who has been researching Nessie since 1973. The most prolific theory of what Nessie is that it is a surviving population of *plesiosaurs* which have been able to survive in Loch Ness. This theory doesn't hold a lot of water, but it is possible that larger marine animals are able to get into the loch via the River Ness. is speculated that animals like dolphins, seals and even the ʌland shark have made their way into the loch periodically.

New Delhi Monkey Man

The New Delhi monkey man could be one of the most infamous incidents in Indian cryptozoology. This peculiar phenomenon began in the early 2000s, during the sultry summer days in New Delhi, India. Residents claimed that they were seeing and even being assaulted by a strange creature. The common description of the creature is of a primate between 4 to 6 feet tall bipedal, with long black fur which covered the body, similar to other bigfoot-like creatures. Soon dubbed the "Monkey Man" this creature was stated to have assaulted several people with its long claws. The creature was seen jumping from roof to roof like a free runner, and attacking individuals outside at night, of which there were many. Because of the heat at night, individuals that slept outside for relief from the heat. Soon after the attacks started to occur there were posses formed to hunt down the creature and end its rampage in their town. Mass hysteria gripped New Delhi, and several residents were injured from running from the monkey man. The sightings stopped as soon as they started. Most think that the creature was a creature like the mande-barung, often seen north of New Delhi. It is hard to differentiate true sightings from misidentifications of real monkeys, because of the mass hysteria that gripped the people of New Delhi. It is possible the monkey man was a misplaced mande-barung who became violent due to the alien environment it found itself in.

Ngoima

The ngoima is a large unknown raptor seen in the Congo. The indigenous cultures of the Congo state that the ngoima is a giant predatory bird with the capacity to carry off human infants and attack adults. One of the first cryptozoologists to study the ngoima was Roy Mackal who obtained a description for the ngoima. The ngoima is a raptor with a wingspan of 9 to 14 feet wide, dark brown to black feathers with darker feathers on the underbelly and beneath the wings, a hooked beak, large talons and legs as large as a human's forearm. The ngoima's main prey source are monkeys that are found in the trees of the Democratic Republic of the Congo. This is similar to the harpy eagle of the Amazon rainforest of South America which primarily preys on monkeys and sloths. Mackal believed that the ngoima could be a crowned eagle, as they are found in the region, but their wingspan is only 4 to 5 feet wide. Another candidate for the ngoima is the martial eagle, found in Sub-Saharan Africa, but their wingspan only reaches about 8 feet wide. Some do think that the ngoima could be a crowned eagle, because that the species has the strength to carry off a large animal. One of the biggest pieces of evidence for the ngoima is the Taung child. This is the fossil of a young *australopithecine* that was killed by an eagle. The eagle that supposedly did the killing was a crowned eagle. It's possible the legend of the ngoima originated \m the crowned eagle and its size was greatly increased due to fear.

Nguma-monene

The nguma-monene is yet another cryptid seen in the Congo. Similar to many other cryptids of the region, the nguma-monene is believed to be a living dinosaur and have aquatic abilities. Translated to "large python" in the Lingala language, the first individuals to encounter the creature were the indigenous people of the Congo. The description of the creature is a serpent 30 to 60 feet long which is mostly seen in the water, with a ridge down its back that many see similar to crocodilians, grey to green colored skin, large scales and a serpent-like head. One of the first cryptozoologists to study the nguma-monene was Roy Mackal, who was one of the first to study the majority of Congolese cryptids. The initial reports told Mackal that the nguma-monene appeared like a large monitor lizard or even crocodilian. Mackel himself stated that the nguma-monene is most likely a new species of giant monitor lizard, which uses the waterways of the Congo to travel. This is what most believe this creature to be; an unknown species of large monitor lizard. The strangest aspect of the nguma-monene is that recently some have speculated that it is a living dinosaur, as most of the other cryptids from this region are believed to be relic dinosaurs. These individuals think the nguma-monene is some type of surviving *spinosaurus* due to the small sail of scales down its back. I myself disagree with this and believe that this cryptid is just a yet to be discovered species of large monitor lizard or giant snake.

Nguoi-rung

The nguoi-rung is one of the most well-known cryptid apes seen in Southeast Asia. Seen primarily in the impenetrable jungles of Vietnam Laos and Cambodia. The translation of nguoi-rung is "buffalo monkey" due to the sheer size of the creature, although it is small in comparison to other unknown apes seen around the globe. The indigenous tribes of Vietnam were the first witnesses to the nguoi-rung. The nguoi-rung was seen as very similar to humans; there are even anecdotal references of nguoi-rung coming out of their forest home and sitting with humans near their fires at night. The nguoi-rung didn't speak, but after a time would just reenter the forest as if they were never there in the first place. The common description of the nguoi-rung is of a bipedal primate about 5 to 7 feet tall with red to black colored fur, long arms, and human-like features. Tales of the nguoi-rung were confined to Vietnam until the 1960s. American G.Is returning from the Vietnam War were coming back with stories of bigfoot-like creatures which lived in the thick forests of Vietnam and even threw rocks at them. The name GIs gave to these creatures were "rock apes". The theories of what the nguoi-rung are vary from surviving Neanderthals, a very archaic tribe of people and even misidentified orangutans, which aren't found on the Asian mainland anymore. One of the most likely theories is that the nguoi-rung are rviving populations of *homo erectus* or *paranthropus*.

Ninki-nanka

The ninki-nanka is an animal that originates from the folklore of Western Africa. The first physical appearance of the ninki-nanka is of a creature with the neck of a giraffe, a horse-like head and the body of a crocodile. Later descriptions are more akin to a monitor lizard or crocodile. The ninki-nanka was a creature that parents would use to scare their children. Soon after that many cryptozoologists thought that the ninki-nanka could be a real-life animal. Soon witnesses started seeing the ninki-nanka as a creature similar to emela-ntouka of the Congo, only without the horn on the snout. Soon there were expeditions to find the creature. One of the most well-known cryptozoologists to pursue the ninki-nanka is Richard Freeman from the Centre for Fortean Zoology. Freeman believed that the ninki-nanka is a giant monitor lizard, inhabiting the rivers of West Africa. Another explanation for the ninki-nanka is that because it is seen with a long neck and horse-like head it is possible that the creature is an aquatic reptilian, similar to many other lake monsters seen throughout the world. One strong possibility that explains the ninki-nanka is that it is like the other living dinosaurs of Africa. It's just folklore from the indigenous tribes that have been misinterpreted as dinosaurs in order to make Africa appear to be a sort of primordial jungle untouched by time.

Nittaewo

The nittaewo is a small unknown primate that is seen in the country of Sri Lanka of Southeast Asia. First mentioned by the indigenous Vedda tribe, the nittaewo was believed to be similar to humans, but since they live in the jungle, were more primitive. There are records of the nittaewo being a violent being and living in complex family groups. The Vedda tribe believed that the nittaewo inhabited the Knuckles Mountain Range in central Sri Lanka. In Vedda folklore the nittaewo are extinct, as they were wiped out by the Vedda. In the late 18th century, the Vedda tribe trapped the nittaewo in a cave and set a pile of brush on fire, suffocating the nittaewo inside. Most held the belief was that the nittaewo was killed even though there was a notion that a male and female nittaewo did escape and survived. The Vedda described the nittaewo as a bipedal human-like primate with long red fur, pointed heels and only 3 feet tall. These were recorded by Frederick Lewis in 1914, who recorded the folklore of the Vedda people. Later cryptozoologists believe the nittaewo was a population of *homo-erectus* that were able to survive in Southern Asia. It is possible that the other unknown bipedal primates seen in Southeast Asia are surviving relatives of the nittaewo that have migrated to more hospitable habitats. Maybe the nittaewo are extinct but their kin still persist in the unexplored jungles of Asia till this day.

Ogopogo

Possibly the most well-known lake monster in Canada, Ogopogo is an aquatic cryptid seen in Lake Okanagan in British Columbia Canada. First seen by the indigenous tribes of Canada, their belief was that Ogopogo was a giant serpent which made Lake Okanagan its home. The description for Ogopogo is similar to the other lake monsters in Canada, a serpentine creature about 20 to 30 feet in length, snake-like head, and smooth dark-colored eel-like skin. Soon after a number of sightings of the creature in the 1920s, national attention was brought to Lake Okanagan and its lake creature. Cryptozoologists saw that there are many similarities of Ogopogo and the other lake monsters seen in Canada like Winnepogo and Igopogo. Even the name of many other lake creatures seen in Canada are derived from the name Ogopogo and is correct due to the similarities of the animals. Similar to Nessie of Scotland and Champ of the U.S Ogopogo soon became an icon for Lake Okanagan and became a cryptozoological celebrity and a pop culture character in British Columbia. There are many theories of what Ogopogo is, from a misidentification of known animals of driftwood to a giant serpent. The most-believed theory is that it is a giant eel similar to the other lake monsters seen from British Columbia to Quebec. This might mean that most of the lake monsters seen in Canada might be the same species or somehow related to one another.

Olitiau

The olitiau is a large bat seen in Cameroon, Africa. The indigenous tribes tell tales of the olitiau; a large nocturnal bat which feeds on local fruits. The description of the olitiau is of a bat with a wingspan of 6 to 12 feet wide with black leathery wings and black fur. The most well-known sighting of an olitiau occurred in 1932 when Ivan T. Sanderson and Gerard Russell were in the sultry jungles of Cameroon when they saw a giant bat. Later Sanderson described the creature as "a black thing the size of an eagle". Most think that the olitiau could be a misidentification of known bats. The problem is that the largest known bat indigenous to Africa is the hammerhead bat, which has a very distinctive head and a wingspan of only about 3 feet, puny when compared to the massive olitiau. The largest known *chiroptera* species is the flying fox of Southeast Asia and has a wingspan of about 4 to 5 feet wide, still very small when compared to the olitiau and on the other side of the globe. One other explanation for the olitiau is a species of bat from 35 million years ago; named the *Witwatia schlosseri* which is from Egypt and was much larger than any known bat today. It is possible the olitiau is a surviving population of these animals, which have made their roosts in the jungles of Cameroon. It is also possible that the olitiau is a close descendant of the genus that has kept its gigantic size.

Onza

The onza is another mysterious cryptid feline seen in the Southwest of the United States and Mexico. The onza has a deep cultural history in Mexico and northern Central America. The first recorded culture to encounter the onza were the Aztecs of Mexico. The Aztecs described the onza as similar to a mountain lion but larger with a lighter, almost gold-colored coat and an even more violent temperament. Legend even states that Montezuma himself had an onza in his own private zoo. The conquistadors who came to Mexico also encountered the onza and stated that they were larger than a puma and a lot more ferocious. The common description for the onza is a feline about 6 feet long, and 2 feet tall at the shoulder, a light-colored coat similar to the puma but usually lighter, a long tail and a very violent temperament. Later settlers in the Southwest encountered the onza and believed they were very dangerous and would attack their livestock and even themselves. Soon enough. by the late 20th century the sightings of the onza stopped. Supposedly, in the 1980s the last onza was killed in Arizona. The carcass was not believed to be any of the indigenous felines in the region. Later examination into the carcass stated it could have been a subspecies of cougar. This has made many suspect the onza was a subspecies of cougar, with a different and lighter coat. Since there aren't any more reports of the onza, it is likely these amazing animals are now extinct.

Orang-bati

The orang-bati is one of the strangest cryptids seen in Southeast Asia. The orange-bati which translates to "batman" originates from the Indonesian island of Seram. The creature is very similar to other cryptids across the world. The natives claim that the orang-bati is a nocturnal aerial creature, with the body of a human and leathery wings. The creature is also said to have a furry monkey-like body. The orang-bati supposedly lives in local volcanoes in the area. It comes down at night to feed on livestock like chickens and small mammals. The orang-bati also supposedly snatches infants and children from their homes at night. The description of the orang-bati is a peculiar one; for any viewers of the *Wizard Of Oz* who remember the flying monkeys, the orang-bati is similar to those creatures. A creature with the body of a monkey with red fur, about 4 to 5 feet tall, and two leathery bat-like wings about 10 to 14 feet wide. The idea of the orang-bati is that they are flying humanoids similar to the ones seen in the U.S, but others think that the orang-bati could be a creature similar or identical to the ahool of Java. It is possible that the orang-bati is a species of giant bat like what the Javan ahool is believed to be. It is also possible that the orang-bati is a misidentification of a flying fox, the largest known extant bat.

Orang-pendek

The orang-pendek is one of the cryptids that is most likely to exist. The orang-pendek originates from the remote regions of Sumatra where the indigenous tribes first told the tales of this creature. The translation for orang-pendek is "forest people," similar to the orangutan that is seen in the same region. The orang-pendek is like many other bigfoot-like creatures seen in the world, except for that it is small in stature. The height of the creature is only around 4 to 5 feet tall. The orang-pendek is seen as a forest protector, much as how First Nations people view the sasquatch. The description of the orang-pendek is of a bipedal primate about 4 to 5 feet tall with red fur, a human-like face, and irregularly pointed heels. The first Europeans to encounter the orang-pendek were Dutch settlers to Sumatra in the 20th century. In the late 20th century this cryptid got worldwide recognition due to the stories of the orang-pendek now being passed to Western researchers. Nowadays the orang-pendek is one of the most well-known cryptids of Southeast Asia. Researchers today have many theories of what the orang-pendek is. In 2003 on the nearby island of Flores the species known as *homo floresiensis* was discovered. This species was a human-relative which only reached around 4 feet tall. This has caused many to believe the orang-pendek is a surviving population of these hominids or a close relative to them.

Owlman

The Owlman is one of those cryptids which is peculiar enough by itself, but when you take into account the phenomena ocurring around it, it just gets weirder and weirder. This beast was first seen in Mawnan, Cornwall, England in the 1970s at a local church and its cemetery. The first sighting of the Owlman occurred in 1976 when a young lady and her parents were on vacation; the young lady saw a strange humanoid figure in the cemetery. Soon enough the creature unwrapped its wings and flew into the air. This started a series of sightings of the creature that locals soon coined the "Owlman." The description of the Owlman is of a humanoid figure with an owl-like head, bird-like legs, wings with brown feathers, and glowing yellow eyes. Along with Owlman sightings there was a rash of peculiar phenomena such as U.F.O. sightings, strange noises coming from radios and T.Vs at night and strange animal attacks. There were also sightings of lake monsters and other cryptids at the same time as this Owlman flap. Some have even made a correlation between the Owlman of England and the Mothman of the United States, as sightings occurred in conjunction with peculiar phenomena. Even the descriptions of the two beings are similar. These correlations might tell us that the Owlman might be like the Mothman and from another world or plane of existence. The more mundane explanation for the Owlman is that it is a misidentification of known large owls or a new species of giant owl found in the British Isles.

Ozark Howler

The Ozark howler may not be an extremely well-known cryptid, but it sure is loud. The story of the Ozark howler started in the small rural towns of Missouri, Arkansas, and other parts of the Ozark Mountains. At night, residents of small rural towns would hear strange vocalizations and believed they were not from any known animal. Soon witnesses saw a creature they couldn't explain. The description of the creature is of a feline about 9 feet long with a long tail, long black fur, and horns on its head, though that aspect of the creature is not seen in all sightings. Also, along with peculiar vocalizations and strange sightings there was also a depredation of local livestock attributed to the creature. The sightings were happening in a great number until in the early 2000s. After that, there were only sporadic sightings of the creature and reports of its vocalization. Most researchers think that the creature is just a made-up hoax. Because of similarities to other unknown felines seen in the U.S., it is possible that the Ozark howler is not a hoax and is related to sightings of other unknown felines seen in the U.S. The reports of the creature having horns on its head could be due to fear and a connection people of the region make due to the correlation of evil mysterious creatures and biblical demons. It is possible that the Ozark howler is an example of modern-day folklore which has created a life of its own.

Paddler

The paddler is a lake monster that is seen in Lake Pend Oreille in Idaho. Lake Pend Oreille is one of the largest lakes in the U.S with a depth of 1,150 feet and a surface area of 148 square miles. Starting in 1944, there were a number of sightings of a large shape in the lake. Most eyewitnesses describe seeing a large wake in the water whose origins were unknown. The description of the creature was a creature about 20 feet long, serpentine, and dark in color. Most who researched the sightings thought that the creature could be similar to the other lake monsters seen in the U.S. Soon the sightings died down in the 1950s, but later in the 1960s a number of other sightings started to occur in the lake. Some of the most recent sightings occurred in the 1980s and in 2007 a photo was published that supposedly depicts the creature. Most think that the photo is too undetailed to see if it is a creature. Later research into the creature brought out a new theory about what the paddler really was. Most think that the paddler is nothing but a submarine that was tested in Lake Pend Oreille during World War II. The United States Navy even had a small base at the end of the lake. where most think the vehicle was docked. Others think that the paddler could be a giant sturgeon. The paddler might be an example of a lake monster being created thanks to overactive imaginations. Sightings after World War II were most likely due to the belief of a creature in the lake and mass hysteria.

Phantom Kangaroos

This is a name used for kangaroos that are seen outside of their normal range. Kangaroos are a marsupial species native to Australia, but these animals are seen in regions far away from their indigenous habitat. Most such sightings originate from the American Midwest. For decades there has been a tradition of kangaroo sightings throughout the Midwestern states. The description of these creatures is of an animal about 4 to 6 feet tall, with red to grey colored fur, long back legs, long tail; the exact description of the kangaroos found in Australia. Most sightings of these creatures occurred in Illinois, Indiana, Wisconsin, and Ohio. One of the most well-known incidents of these creatures occurred in 1974 in Chicago, Illinois. Chicago police officers were looking for a kangaroo and even encountered it. They tried to restrain it, but it attacked them and was able to get away. Due to the number of sightings and the similarities of descriptions, cryptozoologists have concluded that there is a breeding population of kangaroos in the U.S. Midwest. The next question is, where did they come from? Most think they are escapees from circuses and private collections. Loren Coleman thinks that these kangaroos are a misidentification of another cryptid, devil monkeys. The devil monkey has a similar description to a kangaroo so it's possible that some of these kangaroo sightings might actually be these cryptids instead.

Piasa Bird

The piasa bird could be one of the most peculiar creatures that has been seen in the air space above North America. The origins of the piasa bird originated from the oral tradition of the indigenous groups along the Mississippi River. A physical depiction of the piasa bird was discovered as pictographs on bluffs along the Mississippi River near Alton Illinois. Tribes along the Mississippi River thought the piasa bird was a very dangerous aerial creature that could kill people and predated on livestock and other large animals. The piasa is a creature with the head of a feline, with antlers on its head, bird-like wings that stretch about 20 feet, the body of a lion, long serpent tail and long talons on the back feet. The folklore of the piasa bird states that a local chief Ountoga had a dream that showed him how to kill the furious piasa. One day Chief Ountoga took his best warriors to the piasa's lair and using himself as bait was able to lore the piasa out. Once the creature was out the warriors shot bows with poisoned arrows into the piasa's body, killing the creature. Most think this is simple folklore but some think that the piasa bird could be based on a real creature. Possibly a thunderbird or another type of aerial cryptid seen in North America. The piasa bird, if it was truly a thunderbird, can show how the human imagination can create a truly magnificent creature from a more mundane source.

Popelick Monster

The Popelick monster is a local urban legend from Pope Lick Creek in Louisville, Kentucky. Pope Lick Creek is well known due to the large railroad trestle that spans the creek; it is also known for its local unknown creature. The locals near the Pope Lick Trestle state that a malicious creature inhabits the valley beneath it. Known locally as the Popelick monster, it is believed to be a creature like the goatman, seen in other parts of the country. Local residents describe the Popelick monster as a bipedal creature about 5 to 7 feet tall with goat-like legs and tail, human-like torso and head with brown fur. The local legend for the creature is that a circus freak escaped into the woods near the Pope Lick Trestle. Now the creature lures local teens to the trestle where they are killed by oncoming trains. There have been incidents in the past of teens from the area near the trestle being forced to cross the trestle by an unknown force and then meeting their demise by a train, or even by the creature itself. Most do think the story is just a story and is not based on a real creature. Others believe in the notion of goatmen and think this creature to be one of them. The Popelick monster is just a local legend and is most likely not based in reality. I'm not trying to take away from the tragic deaths that have occurred on this trestle but stating that the perpetrator is a goatman is utterly erroneous. These deaths are most likely caused by local teens egging each other on to the trestle then blaming their guilty conscience on an urban legend.

Popobawa

The popobawa is a flying cryptid seen in the African country of Zanzibar and the island of Pemba. First seen in the 1970s, residents of Pemba Island were reporting being assaulted by a nocturnal winged invader that would fly into their windows and attack them. The translation for popobawa is "bat wing" in the local dialect which describes the popobawa fairly well. Supposedly at night residents of the cities of Pemba were under the onslaught of an evil spirit that would enter their domiciles at night in order to attack them and some reports even stated the creature would sexually assault residents. The common description of the popobawa is of a humanoid creature about 3 to 4 feet tall with bat-like wings, red hairless skin, one eye, and long claws. Some of the victims of the popobawa stated that during the attack the popobawa would speak, tormenting the victim and forcing them confess their ordeal to the public. This mass hysteria occurred periodically during the next couple of decades, with some of the most recent occurring in 2007. The locals believed the popobawa was a shetani, an evil spirit. Some later researchers into the popobawa believe that it isn't a spirit, but it could be one of the most horrific political stunts ever used. The popobawa attacks would always correlate to local elections. It has been theorized that the local political party used the mass hysteria of the popobawa in order to gain votes. The attacks by the popobawa are probably a mix of mass hysteria, purposeful deception, and criminal attacks.

Proto-Pygmies

The word proto-pygmy is a name used for unknown humanoid primates seen across the world. The major aspect that differentiates these creatures from other cryptid primates is the size of these creatures. Noted cryptozoologists Mark A. Hall, Ivan T. Sanderson, Patrick Hughye, and Loren Coleman coined this name in order to describe unknown bipedal primates seen in tropical regions along the Equator. There is a plethora of cryptids that are under the name proto-pygmy; these include the orang-pendek, teh-lma, alux, agogwe, ebu-gogo, and batutut. There is a common description for them; a bipedal creature between 3 to 5 feet tall, with fur black to red in color, or primarily red, small proportions, and human-like face. One interesting physical aspect to these creatures, and common in all of them are pointed heels. The possibility of the existence of these animals can be helped by a biological rule called Bergmann's Law, which states that fauna in colder climates grow larger that animals in warmer climates, and these animals are seen in warm climates. The theories of the origin of these creatures are that they are relict populations of hominids like *Authriopecicenes* and *homo-erectus*. One of the other candidates is the *homo-florienciences* due to the fact that many of these proto-pygmy sightings occur on the islands of Southeast Asia.

Queensland Tiger

The Queensland tiger is a large unknown feline-like marsupial seen in Queensland Australia. Most of the reports occur in the jungles of Australia and in and around Queensland Australia. The first culture to report this creature are the Aborigines that called the creature "yarri." The Aborigines saw the yarri as a large marsupial with a body similar to a feline, which is very dangerous to humans and animals. When settlers came to Australia they also encountered the creature; they soon called the creature the Queensland tiger based on the striped coat of the creature. The description of the creature is of a marsupial about the size of a leopard, feline-like head, long streamlined and powerful body, and an orange and black striped coat. The European settlers who came to Australia soon had their livestock taken by a strange animal that they would attribute to the Queensland tiger. After the 1950s the sightings of the creature died down, causing some to think that the beast could now be extinct. Some researchers into the creature believe it is a surviving *thylacine*, a large predatory marsupial, while another theory was that it is a surviving *thylacoleo* or "marsupial lion," which once lived in the areas where the Queensland Tiger was seen. The Queensland tiger's description is a mix of both *thylacoleo* and *thylacine* characteristics so it's possible this animal is another example of a single cryptid created from several other animals. It might be likely that small populations of both *thylacine* and *thylacoleo* were able to survive until the last century.

Ropen

The ropen is one of the less well-known aerial cryptids that is seen in the south Pacific. Seen in New Guinea, this cryptid is seen as being similar to the Kongamato of Africa, as the ropen is seen as a *pterosaur*-like reptilian creature. First seen by the indigenous culture of New Guinea the meaning for ropen is "devil flyer," as it is said to be evil and even feed on human flesh. The tribes of New Guinea believed the ropen would consume human flesh from newly buried graves. The description of the ropen is of a flying reptile with a wingspan of about 12 to 30 feet wide, red scaly skin with bat-like leathery wings, a short tail and a crest on the head. One peculiar aspect of the ropen is that it supposedly emits light from its body, possibly demonstrating bioluminescence qualities. It is believed to be two different ropens, a small animal with a wingspan of about 6 to 12 feet and a larger animal with a wingspan of 20 to 30 feet. It is possible that the smaller is just juvenile ropen, and the larger are the adults of the species. The origins of the ropen may be that they are surviving *pterosaurs* from the Mesozoic era. One candidate could be the Pteranodon of the Cretaceous era. Even with the strong oral history, the scientific plausibility of surviving *pterosaurs* is so low that it's very unlikely but not impossible that the ropen truly are *pterosaurs*. We might have an example of a misidentification of known species or even a new species of large bat that has bioluminescent characteristics.

Rougarou

The rougarou is a peculiar canine creature seen in southern Louisiana. Similar to the loup-garou, the rougarou is believed to be a creature that dwells in the bayous of Louisiana. One thing that separates the rougarou from other cryptids is that it has several versions of the creature, most think about three different versions. One version is of a werewolf-like creature that for 101 days turns into a bipedal canine about 6 to 8 feet tall with brown fur and when cut by a blade the curse moves onto a new person. This legend comes from the French Cajuns that settled in Louisiana and brought their own legends. The second is of an astral spirit-like being that is seen as a bayou devil or demon. Most see this version connected to Voodoo and black magic. This version of the animal is what many Cajuns think the loup-garou is. Another version is of a creature similar to a bigfoot-like creature or bipedal canine-like creature that is entirely physical and non-metamorphic. Most see this creature as like the loup-garou, which is seen in the same region that the rougarou is seen. The main difference between the rougarou and the loup-garou is that the loup-garou is believed to be more spiritual while the rougarou is more physical in nature. The theories of what the rougarou is varies from a bigfoot-like primate creature to a werewolf-like creature. Most Cajuns of Louisiana do believe that it is like the loup-garou and is a canine. It is possible that the rougarou is just another example of a bipedal canine.

Row

The row is a rather peculiar cryptid seen in the South Pacific. In the 1930s honeymooners Charles and Leona Miller were in the jungles of New Guinea, where they supposedly discovered a new tribe. Called the Kirrirri, they had an oral tradition of a giant reptile which inhabited the local jungles, and which they called the row. The indigenous people used rudimentary tools made from the body parts of the creature. The Kirrirri led the couple into the nearby swamps where they supposedly killed a 40-foot-long reptile resembling a dinosaur. The Millers described the row as an amalgamation of different animals; 40 feet long with a long neck and tail, a turtle-like beak, a frill along the neck, plates down its back, and a group of spikes on its tail. Soon the couple spread their story of a living dinosaur in the jungles of New Guinea. Later researchers believe that the whole story is a fictional story. This is due to that the tribe the couple describe the "Kirrirri" never existed, and the description of the row is very strange. The row itself is an amalgamation of different dinosaur species which had starkly different physical attributes. During the 1920s and 30s there was a dinosaur craze, and it appears that the Millers wanted to add to that. The row can be seen as proof against the idea of living dinosaurs. Even with the outlandish description the row was at first believed to be real. It was only through later scrutiny was it proven that the Millers were being fictitious. Makes you wonder, what cryptids now are like the row, just good stories?

Salawa

The salawa is a canine cryptid seen in Egypt. The name salawa translates to "scary wolf" due to the salawa being so violent and it being a canine. Using the name salawa to describe this creature originated in the 1960s but some think that a creature similar to it has been in Egypt since ancient times. Named Sha, this was a canine that was connected to Seth the god of disorder and destruction. The description of Sha was of a slender canine with large ears, long legs, and a striped coat. It is thought that this creature could be based on the real life salawa. The salawa originates from the 1960s when a series of attacks started to occur in southern Egypt especially in agricultural towns and large sugar cane fields. The creature believed to be perpetuating these attacks was a canine about 4 to 5 feet tall at the shoulder, with a striped coat, long legs, sloped back, large head and ferocious teeth and claws. Soon the attacks started to fall off, but they did leave several deaths, and a deep fear of this creature. These attacks did occur again in the 1990s and stopped soon after, just like the 1960s incident. Most think that the salawa was a striped hyena which found its way into human habitations. Some other researchers think it is a misidentification of a fennec fox. Others think that the salawa is a new species of canine that lives in the wilds of Egypt.

Sasquatch

The sasquatch is a large bipedal primate seen in the Northern part of North America. The name sasquatch originates from a schoolteacher. Ivan T. Burns from British Columbia, Canada. Burns investigated the oral tradition of several indigenous peoples of the Pacific Northwest, which all had a tradition of human-like beings living in the woods. Names for such creatures varied from "oma," "skookum," and "kushtaka," which meant either wild man or man of the woods. Soon Burns turned these names into one name he called sasquatch. Since then, that has been` the name used for any large hairy human-like primates seen in the Pacific Northwest, though it is used in other parts of the U.S. The description of the sasquatch is of a bipedal primate about 6 to 9 feet tall, with black to red fur, large feet, human-like face, long arms, barrel chest and heavy brow ridge. There is a plethora of evidence for this animal, from footprint casts, videos to thousands of eyewitness accounts. The sasquatch of the Pacific Northwest and Canada are the same creatures known as bigfoot in other regions of the U.S. Sasquatch is just another colloquial name for the large bipedal primates seen in North America. Just like bigfoot, sasquatch is believed to be a surviving population of giant ape called *gigantopithecus* that was found in China during the Pleistocene epoch. One difference between the sasquatch of Canada and the bigfoot of the U.S is that sasquatch are believed to be a little larger than bigfoot seen in lower latitudes.

Sea Serpents

The sea serpent is a creature which features in all to most maritime cultures throughout recorded history. From Japan to the U.S to Greece to Australia, there are sightings of unknown marine animals periodically throughout history. Most scientists believe that these sightings are simple misidentifications of known animals, overactive imaginations or just stories created to entertain others. Well, this was until when "Father of Cryptozoology," Bernard Heuvelmans, began to study sea serpent sightings in the early 20th century. Soon Heuvelmans noticed that descriptions of these creatures were very similar. He developed a hypothetical classification system for these animals. This consisted of 9 species of sea serpents; the long-necked, the merhorse, many-humped, super otter, many-finned, super eels, marine saurian, father of all turtles and yellow belly. All these hypothetical species have their own explanations. For Heuvelmans the long necked are *plesiosaurs*, merhorses are an unknown pinniped, many humped are a variant of cetacean, super otter is another unknown cetacean or large marine mammal, many-finned an unknown cetacean or aquatic arthropods, super eels are giant eels, marine saurians are aquatic reptiles, father of all turtles is a giant turtle and yellow belly an unknown marine mammal. All of these species are just hypothetical, but it doesn't necessarily mean they aren't real. Thanks to the mystery of our oceans, it is possible that some of these species do exist and are waiting for us to discover them.

Selma

Seen in Lake Seljord in Norway, which covers an area of 276.1 miles square and a depth of about 400 to 500 feet deep. Selma is believed to be a lake monster living in this lake. There is a long history of an unknown species dwelling in it; sightings go back to the 1750s. A resident near the lake was walking along the shore when he was suddenly attacked by a large animal from the lake. The description of the creature appears to have altered over the years. Some of the first witnesses described the creature as being similar to the mythological merhorse of European folklore; a creature with a horse-like body, and head and fish tail. Later sightings describe a creature more akin to the Ogopogo of Canada, a serpentine animal about 40 to 60 feet long with dark colored skin. Researchers into Selma believe this difference is due to that the first description is a less realistic representation of the creature. The most prolific researcher into Selma is Swedish cryptozoologist Jan Ove Sundberg, who coined the name Selma for the creature. Thanks to the number of sightings and fame of Selma, Seljord, the municipality where the lake is located put Selma on its coat of arms in 1989. It is believed that Selma is a giant freshwater eel that has survived in the lake for centuries.

Sesimite

The sesimite, also spelled sisimite, is a large sasquatch-like cryptid primate seen in the tropical jungles of South and Central America, especially in Guatemala and Mexico. The indigenous tribes of the region like the Chorti tribe have been telling tales of this creature for centuries. The description of the sesimite is of a creature about 6 to 9 feet tall, humanoid with long red to black fur, no real neck and human-like face. The question is, how did these creatures get to South America? I have a theory that early hominins and the primates that would have evolved into hominids in Africa were translocated in South America via rafts and floating debris. Most believe that monkeys first got to South America about 40 million years ago. Hominids first evolved about 2.5 million years ago, so could it be possible that the primates that found themselves in South America could have evolved into creatures very similar to the hominids of Africa via convergent evolution? It could be that the hominids in Africa like *homo-erectus* sailed to South America by island hopping and the strong currents of the Atlantic. Paleontologists do think that *homo-erectus* did sail in the Pacific so could they also sail across the Atlantic. This could explain the sightings of human-like primates in South America today. It is also possible that these primates are actually the same as the North American bigfoot but due to environmental influencers have adapted morphologically in order to survive in the jungles of South America.

Sharlie

Lake Payette in western Idaho supposedly harbors a large aquatic cryptid. Lake Payette has a depth of about 392 feet and is 5,300 acres in area. The history of the lake monster which lives in these waters began in the 1920s when several local loggers and railroad workers started to see a huge unidentified animal in the lake. These were some of the first recorded sightings of the creature but before settlers came into the region the indigenous tribes told stories of an evil spirit being in the lake. Later in 1944 the first widespread sightings of the creature started to occur, when 30 witnesses saw a creature in the lake that they soon nicknamed "Slimy Slim." The sightings were so believed to be true and prolific that *Time Magazine* published an article about the creature in 1944. The description of the creature is of a creature about 30 feet long with smooth skin, crocodilian-like nose, and long neck with a large body similar to a *plesiosaur*. The name Sharlie originated in 1954 from an individual from Virginia who gave the name as part of a contest to rename the creature. Since then, Sharlie has become an attraction at the nearby McCall, Idaho, a resort town that is centered around Lake Payette. Some have speculated that Sharlie, like some other lake monsters, was created in order to bring tourists to the region. If Sharlie is a real animal, it is likely that it is a giant species of fish or eel.

Sheepsquatch

This is a rather peculiar name for a rather peculiar cryptid. The sheepsquatch is a cryptid seen in the Appalachian Mountains of West Virginia. This creature has a more recent history than several other creatures of the U.S. The first recorded sightings of this creature originate in the 1990s when residents of West Virginia started to see a bipedal, white-coated creature that they soon nicknamed "The White Thing." Even with recent history there are some who claim the legend of this creature goes back to when settlers first came to the Appalachians. Sheepsquatch is described as a bipedal creature with white fur, two goat-like horns, a goat-like head, hooves, and long claws. The belief in this creature is strong but the probability of this creature actually existing is low to nonexistent. There isn't any evolutionary or biological precedent for such a creature existing. This cryptid is most likely a figment of collective cultural imagination similar to the goatman and Jersey devil. This creature was probably created thanks to combined characteristics too. Most likely bigfoot sightings are interpreted as a sheepsquatch thanks to the folklore of this creature. The goat-like appearance of this animal most likely is formed from the strong religious sentiments in the region. The horns and goat-like face probably appear thanks to the description of biblical demons and the devil. Sheepsquatch can help show us how our imaginations and preconceived notions can form an animal that isn't based in science but belief and superstition.

Shunka Warakin

The shunka warakin is a strange canine-like cryptid seen in the American Midwest. The lore of the shunka warakin originates from the Iowa Tribe where the name translates to "the carries off dogs" as this particular cryptid has a taste for canines. The shunka warakin is widespread from Iowa to Montana, where most sightings occur for this creature. The description of this creature is of a canine-like mammal about 3 to 4 feet tall at the shoulder, high shoulders, wolf-like head, hyena-like tail, a sloped back, and brown to grey fur. Most see it as a hybridization of wolf and hyena features. The most well-known incident that has to do with the shunka warakin occurred in the late 1800s in Montana. A man named Israel Hutchins shot a peculiar creature on his land in Montana. Years later the stuffed body was put on display as a local store but was later lost. A relative of the Hutchins family studied the animal and named it "Ringdocus." He thought that the creature could be a prehistoric hyena which went extinct in the U.S around 780,000 years ago called *chasmaporthetes*. Most modern researchers agree that the shunka warakin might be a population of relit *chasmaporthetes*, as both of their physical descriptions are very similar. The sightings of shunka warakin have greatly diminished in recent time but there are still sporadic sightings of hyena-like animals in the Midwest. It could be possible there are still extant hyenas in North America to this day.

Sirrush

The story of the sirrush started in 1902 when the German archaeologist Robert Koldewey unearthed a part of the ancient city of Babylon. Named the Ishtar Gate this gate was erected in the 6th century B.C.E. The gate depicted several animals that could have been found in the areas around Babylon, well except for one. This creature was known as a sirrush or "dragon," which was thought to be a Biblical dragon that was connected to their gods. The sirrush was very different from anything that should be in ancient Babylon; a reptilian creature with long legs, neck, and tail, scaly skin, curved horns protruding out of an elongated the head, and large bird-like talons. Scientists who studied the animal believe it is a depiction of a mythological animal or even the creature could represent dinosaur fossils that the Babylonians could have found themselves. But other researchers, including Robert Koldewey, think that the sirrush could be a real animal and not a fictional one. Since the sirrush is depicted next to real animals, this might demonstrate that the Babylonians believed the sirrush was a real animal and not a fictitious monster. They theorize that the sirrush could be a surviving dinosaur, possibly a *sauropod* species or even a *hadrosaur* species which had been able to live into recorded history.

Skinwalker

The skinwalker is a being from the oral tradition of the Navajo tribe of the American Southwest. The legend of the skinwalker states that the skinwalker is a shaman who has the ability to shapeshift into an animal. For this to occur the individual has to wear the skin of whichever animal they wish to turn into. The most common animal that these beings turn into are wolves or wolf-like canines. Native American state that the skinwalker is a formidable foe since they have the ferocity of an animal and the cunning and intelligence of a human. Though this animal is sometimes considered a purely fictional animal, many individuals that state that they see this being. Even if the skinwalker was to be real, others say they lie outside the views of cryptozoology. I agree with this statement to a degree. The metamorphic elements of the skinwalker are too fantastical to be analyzed by the science of cryptozoology but the other elements might be worth studying. Most witnesses of skinwalkers describe upright canines or even bigfoot-like creatures. It is possible that these sightings are really of other cryptids such as bigfoot and bipedal canines. It is possible that similar to the werewolf legends of Europe possibly being based on sightings of bipedal canines, this might be occurring here as well. So even though the stories of the skinwalker are very fantastic it is possible that they are based on actual biological species. Just that these species are not yet identified themselves either.

Skunk Ape

This is a regional name for a bigfoot-like creature used in the American south, especially in Florida. The name skunk ape originated from Florida in the 1990s when there were several sightings of a peculiar primate creature in their local woods and swamps. Soon the name "Skunk Ape" was coined due to the horrid smell of the animal, witnesses describe the smell as similar to a decomposing body or to a sulfur odor. The usual description of the skunk ape is very similar to the sasquatch of the Pacific Northwest; a bipedal primate about 6 to 8 feet tall with red to black colored fur, long arms, human-like face and large feet. The best evidence for this creature is the Myakka photo which was taken in 2000 by an elderly couple. The photo depicts a large bipedal primate in the backyard of the couple. Most who have studied the photo believe that it does show a real creature, but one which is still unknown. Researchers into the skunk ape believe that it is the same animal as bigfoot. Others do think that the sightings can be attributed to escaped primates like orangutans and chimps. It is also speculated that the skunk ape isn't a bigfoot at all but more like a Nape. This is due to witnesses seeing more anthropoid ape species in the Florida swamps. The skunk ape is most likely just a bigfoot but one that has adapted morphologically due to the environment it lives in.

Stronsay Beast

The Stronsay Beast is one of the most well-known instances of a globster. The story of the Stronsay beast started in September of 1808 when John Pace was walking on the shore of Stronsay Island in the Orkney Islands. This is where he discovered a large carcass that was different from any other that has been seen in the area, or really anywhere else for the matter. The description of the carcass is one that appeared to have a long neck and tail, 55 feet long with 3 pairs of flippers on the body with bristles going down its back and dark smooth skin. After the carcass was discovered, members of the Natural History Society went to Stronsay and stated they didn't know what the creature could be. Later Scottish anatomist Dr. John Barclay gave the animal that washed on the shores of Stronsay the name "*Halsydrus*" which means "sea snake". At the time, the belief was that the creature that washed up on shore was a sea serpent. Later researchers into the Stronsay beast believe that the creature could be a misidentification of a basking shark or oarfish. Some researchers like Bernard Heuvelmans also believe that the creature was another known species of animal, the basking shark. Even with most believing this creature to be a known species, there are still others that believe the creature could have been a new species of cetacean or even a real-life sea serpent

Surrey Puma

The Surrey puma is the predecessor to many other cryptid felines seen in Great Britain. The Surrey puma was first seen in the late 1950s to early 1960s when there was a rash of livestock depredation and sightings of a large jet-black feline in the area around Surrey, England. Livestock like sheep and goats were soon being killed by an unknown predator, attributed to a feline due to the way the animals were being killed. One of the first instances of livestock depredation was on Bushylease Farm in 1964 where a steer was killed by an unknown predator. This is also when the name 'Surrey Puma" was created by the press. The description of the Surrey puma is very similar to other unknown felines seen in England. The description is of a jet-black cat about 6 feet long, with a long tail, rounded ears, and otherwise very similar to a black panther. The authorities of Surrey believed that the Surrey puma was an escaped exotic cat from a private owner. Sightings of the Surrey puma persisted until the 1980s, when a number of other large cats were being seen in the countryside of the United Kingdom. Some researchers into the Surrey puma think that this creature could be related to the many other large cats seen in England like the Beast of Exmoor and Beast of Bodmin Moor. It appears that the Surrey puma was just the first of a line of cryptid felines later spotted in the U.K. The most likely origins of the Surrey puma is that it is an escaped exotic pet from a private owner in Britain.

Tasmanian Blob

This is where the name globster first originated, by Ivan T. Sanderson. This jelly-like blob was first discovered in Tasmania in 1962. Many individuals who saw this creature believed that it was a sea monster or a carcass of a sea serpent. The physical description of the Tasmanian Blob was a gelatin-like heap of flesh with no real discernible shape or species of origin, about 20 feet wide and 5 to 10 tons in weight. Soon after the discovery of the creature it was deduced that it was the remains of a whale. Even though this particular instance proved to be just a misidentification of a known animal, it led to the widespread study of anomalous carcasses which wash up on shores around the world. Soon the famous explorer and cryptozoologist Ivan T. Sanderson studied the Tasmanian Blob and led him to coin the name "Globster" to describe unknown biological materials which many think originate from an unknown source. Even though many instances of these organic masses prove to have come from a known source, there are a few which prove to be inconclusive. Even though the Tasmanian Blob was eventually proven to be a known species, it has had a profound and lasting effect on cryptozoology and the study of unknown aquatic animals around the world, from which we can still learn today.

Tatzelwurm

This is one of the most well-known of Europe's cryptids. This cryptid is seen in the Alps of Austria and Switzerland. Tatzelwurm means "clawed worm"; the folklore of this alpine creature goes back to the mid-1700s when some of the first sightings were reported. This sighting of the tatzelwurm which occurred in 1778 was supposed to be so frightening that the eyewitness later died from a heart attack due to the experience. The description of the tatzelwurm is of an elongated lizard-like reptile about 2 to 8 feet long, with two front legs and no back limbs, long claws, grey-colored scaled skin, and a cat-like head. The belief at the time was that the tatzelwurm was a real-life dragon living in the high alpine regions of the Alps. The tatzelwurm has been an important aspect of the Alps culture and folklore since they were first sighted in the region. The tatzelwurm is a famous cryptid of Europe due to the number of sightings and also the number of hoaxes of this beast. The belief is that the tatzelwurm is now extinct as there hasn't been a confirmed sighting since the early 20th century. There have been several theories of what the tatzelwurm was. Some have theorized that the tatzelwurm was an unknown species of salamander or species of lizard possibly related to the American gila monster. There is a species called the worm lizard, which is a reptile with only two upper limbs. It is possible the tatzelwurm was a gigantic example of one of these species.

Teh-lma

The teh-lma is an unknown species of ape seen in the foothills of the Himalayan mountains. Unlike the more well-known cryptid that is seen in the Himalayas the yeti but the teh-lma is believed to be much smaller than the yeti. The first culture to encounter the teh-lma were the indigenous Nepalese people. Their belief was that the teh-lma was a smaller variant of the yeti which lived in the tropical forests of the lowlands around the Himalayas. The description of the teh-lma is of a bipedal primate around 3 to 5 feet tall. with black to silver colored fur, long arms, and pointed heels. One of the first westerners to write about the teh-lma was the American naturalist Gerald Russell in 1954. Gerald Russell who encountered a teh-lma himself in 1958, concluded that this creature is a smaller variant of the yeti, a creature indigenous to the sub-alpine tropical valleys of the Himalayas. This is the same conclusion to which several cryptozoologists have come; the teh-lme is a subspecies of the yeti which has become adapted to a lower alpine existence. Even Loren Coleman believes that the teh-lma could be related to the many other proto pygmies seen in Southeast Asia like the nittaewo, batutut, nguoi-rung, and the mandi-barung. It is also possible that the teh-lma isn't related to the yeti at all and that stories of the teh-lma help create the viewpoint that the yeti is an unknown hominid, while later DNA testing has shown the yeti is actually a species of bear.

Tessie

Also known as Tahoe Tessie, this is a large lake monster seen in Lake Tahoe, situated between Nevada and California. Lake Tahoe is the largest lake in the Sierra Nevada mountains and second deepest in the U.S, with a depth of 1,645 feet deep and a surface area of 191 square miles. Stories of a creature dwelling in the lake originate from the indigenous tribes of the Paiute and Washoe tribes. They believed that a large serpent lived in the lake and would kill any who entered its domain. The description of the animal is of a serpentine creature from 10 to 60 feet long, black to dark blue in color, and with a serpent-like head. Some of the first documented sightings occurred in the 1950s when several residents including police officers began seeing a strange shape in the lake. Later in the 1980s there were several more sightings of the creature. This is when the creature started to get recognition. The sightings became so numerous that a hotline was created in order to deal with all of them. The sightings of Tessie still go on till this day. Most believe that the sightings of Tessie are misidentifications of logs and animals in the lake or natural phenomena and mass hysteria. Others have hypothesized that Tessie could be a giant eel or sturgeon that lives in the lake.

Thetis Lake Monster

This is a peculiar aquatic cryptid seen in a lake in British Columbia, Canada. Thetis Lake is only around 86 acres in size. The first sightings of this creature occurred on August 22, 1972; two young local teens stated that a creature emerged from the lake and chased them. The young men described the creature as a humanoid reptilian creature about 5 to 6 feet tall with silver scales, webbed hands and feet, and a reptilian face. Most see a similarity of this creature's description to the monster from the movie *The Creature From the Black Lagoon*. The local authorities investigated the sighting, as did even the Royal Canadian Mounted Police. The investigators came to the conclusion that the boys saw a real creature, but exactly what that creature was remains unknown. Two days after the first sighting two men saw a similar creature on the opposite side of the lake. Most authorities at the time believed that the creature was a misidentification of an exotic pet that escaped their private collector. Later researchers think that the lake creature could be a species of bipedal reptilian creature. It is most likely that the Thetis Lake monster was just an escaped exotic pet and due to the popularity of *The Creature From the Black Lagoon* it was altered into an even more ferocious looking beast.

Thunderbirds

This is a group of large avian cryptids which have been seen throughout North America for centuries. The first cultures to speak of this animal were the many indigenous tribes of the U. S. The Native American tribes have an oral tradition of a giant bird that when it flaps its wings it causes thunder, hence the name Thunderbird. At first, most folklorists assume this legend is describing a fictitious monster or a misidentification of known birds, but cryptozoologists have questioned these ideas. When whites started to settle in North America, they started to see and describe an animal very similar to the native American thunderbird. The description of these creatures are of a bird with a wingspan of 10 to 30 feet wide, with squared wings, and black to brown feathers. Most eyewitnesses report seeing a white ring around the animal's neck. Suddenly in the 20th century there were several waves of sightings of these animals in the American Midwest and southwest. The most well-known incidents with thunderbirds occurred in 1977 in Lawndale, Illinois. What occurred is that 10-year-old Marlon Lowe was playing in his yard when suddenly a giant black bird reached down at him and picked him up, carrying him about 20 feet until it eventually let him go. Paleontology shows a precedent for large raptor-like birds. In North America during the Pleistocene the teratorns ruled the skies. Teratorns were large eagle-like birds with wingspans of up to 20 feet. It is possible that these birds exist today hiding in plain sight above our unknowing heads.

Thylacine

The thylacine scientific name *Thylacinus cynocephalus* was a large predatory marsupial indigenous to Australia and Tasmania. Colloquially known by the names Tasmanian wolf or Tasmanian tiger (due to its striped coat), it was the largest predator native to Tasmania until European settlers came to the region in the 1800s. When their sheep were going missing, they blamed the thylacine for the killings. A bounty was put on the thylacines' head and in 1930 the last-known wild thylacine was shot and killed. The last known thylacine died in 1936 at the Hobart Zoo, and the species officially recognized as extinct. Later residents in Tasmania started to see the thylacine, causing some to believe that it had not been hunted to extinction. Local authorities and governmental bodies investigated the sightings. The description of the animal which people were seeing was of a canine-like marsupial about 6 feet long with a wolf-like head, orange and black striped coat. and long tail, the exact description of the "extinct" thylacine. Most sightings of the thylacine occur in the remote hills and jungles of Tasmania and the rural dirt tracks where individuals see the creature cross. There is a litany of film and photos of supposed thylacines that have left zoologists scratching their heads. Even today, there have been several instances of livestock depredation in the area which are blamed on the tiger due to the lack of any other indigenous large carnivores. So it appears that the thylacine might still dwell in Tasmania today.

Tsuchinoko

The tsuchinoko is a creature from Japanese folklore. For hundreds of years the Japanese have told stories of the tsuchinoko, a peculiar snake. The translation of the name means "hammer's spawn," but there are numerous other names for this creature from different regions of Japan. The name tsuchinoko is primarily used in western Japan while the name bachi hebi is used in northern Japan. Even with the many names, the description of the animals remains consistent from region to region and through the centuries of the sightings. The description is of a snake about 2 to 4 feet long, a wide body compared to a slender head and tail, dark brown to black in color – and venomous. The legends of the tsuchinoko state that the animal can jump a couple of feet and even spit venom like a cobra. This description originates from *Kojiki*, a book from around the 8th century AD about ancient Japan and its many beliefs. The tsuchinoko has in recent years become a pop culture character in Japan. Most believe that the tsuchinoko is a yet-to-be discovered snake species, possibly even a variety of cobra. Some think that it is possible that the enigma may never be solved, since a depletion of reports of the animal in modern times may indicate that the tsuchinoko is now extinct.

U-28 Sea Monster

The U-28 sea monster is not a type of cryptid in and of itself, it is a name given to a particular cryptid incident. The story of the U-28 creature begins July 30, 1915, when the German U-boat sunk the British steamer *Iberian* in the North Atlantic. Soon after the U-boat torpedoed the *Iberian*, the ship sank and then exploded. That is when the crew on the U-28 saw a truly terrifying sight. The explosion on the *Iberian* caused a giant unknown animal to be thrust out of the water right into the air. The crew on the U-boat including the captain described the creature as resembling a giant crocodile. They described the creature as being about 60 feet long with a long crocodile-like head, four long flippers, a long tail with dark colored skin. Soon the animal got away and swam in a way similar to a reptile. After that there weren't any other sightings of the creature. The most widely held theory is that the creature is a marine reptile known as a *mosasaur* from the Mesozoic era. Then the question is why is it in the area? A possible explanation is that the creature has learned that when a ship sinks it can easily consume dead sailors and others in the water. It is possible the animal came to the wreck to feed and then was thrust out of hiding by the explosion. The U-28 sea monster just might be the most famous sighting of a living marine reptile in history.

Ucumar

The ucumar is an unknown humanoid primate seen in South America. This cryptid primate is primarily seen along the western part of South America, especially in Chile and Argentina. The ucumar also known as the ucu is seen primarily in the mountainous and jungles of the Andes Mountains in Chile and Argentina. The first recorded sightings of the ucumar occurred in 1958 when residents near Santiago Chile reported a giant human-like ape in the area. The description of the ucumar is of a bipedal primate about 6 to 8 feet tall, with black to grey colored fur, long claws, and very human-like in appearance. The most well-known aspect of the ucumar is its bad attitude towards equines. There are stories of horses in the Andes Mountains being attacked and killed by this creature. Possibly, this could mean that the animal is territorial and sees horses as intruding on their domain. Most individuals who see the animal think that it is an unknown primate, similar to the North American sasquatch. Most scientists and authorities believe that the ucumar is a misidentification of the spectacled bear, a large ursine species found in the same areas the ucumar is seen. This explanation is not very likely, as the spectacled bear is much smaller than what the ucumar is described as, and the fact that witnesses describe the ucumar as walking bipedally, not just standing erect. It appears the ucumar is just another instance of an unknown bipedal primate in South America.

Vampires

Even though the Hollywood version of the vampire is completely folklore, this menacing creature can still help bring light to the shadows of the unknown. The modern view of the vampire started from Bram Stoker's novel *Dracula*. This title was inspired from the 15th century Romanian ruler Vlad the Impaler. This has made this version of the vampire a modern phenomenon. Most researchers into this creature believe the notion of vampiric activity was formed due to that blood is pushed out of the body during decomposition and the over-sensational superstitions of the period. I have included this creature in this book simply because of the many cultures which have stories of humans and animals that drink blood. These include the aswang of the Philippines to the chupacabra of Latin America. These legends help show how widespread this idea is and how much they are regarded. I am not insinuating that vampires exist or have existed, but the idea of a vampire has persisted for centuries and throughout a plethora of cultures. This demonstrates how ideas can last longer than the people that first made them. This is especially important to cryptozoology – the belief in monsters is widespread through many cultures. Vampires were created from the minds of uninformed and frightened individuals. This phenomenon still happens today, demonstrating that fear and a lack of knowledge can still create monsters, monsters which live in the human psyche and not some unexplored distant forest.

Veo

The veo is a large and unknown insectivore seen on the Rinca Island in Indonesia. The veo was first seen by the indigenous people of the island. They thought that the veo is a mammal about the size of a horse but with armored plating. The veo inhabits the lush jungles of the island and consumes insects primarily ants. The oral tradition about the veo states that if humans get too close to the veo, it will rear up on its hind legs and claw the individuals harassing it. The description of the veo is of a mammal about 6 to 8 feet long, around 2 feet tall with armored sections on its flanks and along the back, a canine-like head, long claws on all four feet, long coarse brown fur the belly, and a short armored tail. Most scientists see a similarity of the veo to the pangolin, which are indigenous to Asia and Africa. The one problem with that is that the largest known species of pangolin is only about 4.5 feet long and native to Africa. Another candidate for the veo is a giant extinct pangolin that was found in Pleistocene-era Borneo, which was about 8 feet long. This has caused many cryptozoologists, even Karl Shuker, to theorize that the veo seen in Rinca is the same animal as the extinct pangolin found in Borneo.

Vouroupatra

The vouroupatra is a large unknown terrestrial avian species that is seen on the island of Madagascar. The first culture to encounter the vouroupatre were the indigenous populations of Madagascar. Their oral tradition states that the vouroupatra is a giant and elusive flightless bird which lives in the jungles of the island. The description of the vouroupatre is of a large bird about 6 to 8 feet tall with long neck brown feathers and very similar to the African ostrich. This description is similar to the moa of New Zealand, though there isn't a discernible connection between them. The first westerner to encounter the vouroupatra was the first French governor of Madagascar, Etienne de Flacourt, in 1658. After that there are not many documented sightings of the vouroupatra. After the mid-19th century there were no recorded sightings of any vouroupatra at all. This lack of sightings makes cryptozoologists to believe this creature had already gone extinct at that point. One likely candidate for the vourupatra is the extinct elephant bird, a giant 10-foot-tall flightless bird found in Madagascar in the Pleistocene era. It is possible that the vouroupatra was a cultural memory of the elephant bird which was able to survive into recorded history. Another possibility is that the voutupatra is a population of elephant birds that miraculously survive today in the remote recess of Madagascar.

Waheela

The waheela is a large cryptid canid seen in the northern parts of Alaska and Canada. Seen primarily near the Arctic Circle, the first people to tell stories of the waheela are the indigenous Inuits. Their stories state that the waheela is a giant wolf-like creature with white fur and that it is much more ferocious than a regular wolf. Another aspect that differentiates the waheela from the wolf is that the waheela doesn't move in packs but are solitary canines. The description of the waheela is of a wolf about 6 to 9 feet long, about 5 feet tall at the shoulder, a bear-like body, white fur, and long canines. One of the first researchers to report on the waheela is Ivan T. Sanderson, who recorded a sighting from an individual he only calls "Frank." In the 1940s Frank met a waheela on a hunting trip in Canada; he described the creature as a mix of wolf and bear with white fur. Most researchers believe the waheela to be just a gigantic form of wolf. On the other hand, Ivan T. Sanderson developed the theory that the waheela isn't a wolf at all but an extinct genus of carnivora called an *amphicyon*. Also known as the "bear dog," these carnivores were the last known ancestors of both canines and bears. This caused these animals to display a mix of both canine-like and bear-like characteristics. These animals were supposed to have gone extinct 5 million years ago, but it could be possible that a small population of these creatures were able to survive in the higher latitudes of Canada and Alaska, thanks to the larger prey species and the lower human population density.

Waitoreke

The waitoreke is a small semi-aquatic mammal seen in New Zealand. Seen primarily near bodies of water on the South Island, the waitoreke is believed to be an unknown species of otter or beaver. The first individuals to see the waitoreke were the indigenous Maori people of New Zealand. The Maori thought that the waitoreke was an animal which spent most of its time in the water but lived on the land. The description of the waitoreke is of a mammal about 1 to 2 feet long with brown fur and webbed feet. One of the first Europeans to hear about the waitoreke was Captain James Cook in the late 1700s.Later settlers gave the waitoreke several nicknames like "New Zealand otter," "New Zealand beaver," and "New Zealand platypus," due to the similarities of the waitoreke with these animals. The waitoreke is still seen today, but most believe that the animal is a lot rarer now because of habitat loss. There are many theories put forward to explain what the waitoreke is. One theory states the waitoreke is an unknown otter or beaver, which would be amazing, as New Zealand does not have any known indigenous extant terrestrial mammals. Some even believe the waitoreke could be an unknown monotreme, an egg-laying mammal like the platypus, which has been able to hide in New Zealand. Another hypothesis is that the waitoreke is a totally new type of mammal, which has evolved in New Zealand on its own and only resembles otters and beavers due to convergent evolution.

Wampus Cat

The wampus cat is a cryptid feline from Native American folklore. The original story of the wampus cat originates from the Cherokee tribe, their folk stories state that a Cherokee woman wished to spy on the elders of the tribe. To do this the woman disguised herself as a cougar and watched the elders, but she was soon caught. For this crime the tribal medicine man turned the women into a ravenous black, similiar to a cougar. From then on, this woman was to roam the Appalachian Mountains, feeding on any unwitting traveler in the woods. Even though this occurred hundreds of years ago, there are still sightings of a creature similar to this one today. Though the name "wampus" is used throughout the Appalachians as a descriptor for an animal that's identity is unknown, this particular use of wampus is used to describe a feline species. The modern witnesses of the wampus cat describe the creature as a feline about 6 to 8 feet long with jet-black fur and a large head. These sightings occur primarily in the Appalachian Mountains and the Ozarks. These animals are blamed for the depredation of livestock throughout the farms of this region. It is a possibility that this animal is the same animal as the many other *panthera atrox* seen in North America. The wampus cat might just be another name for the myriad of black cats seen in the United States. The wampus cat most likely is a melanistic cougar. The black cats being seen today are most likely the basis for the legend of the Cherokee catwoman.

Werewolf

Werewolves or also known as lycanthropes are another one of those creatures which have been in several cultures across the world for centuries. The folklore around werewolves states that a werewolf is a regular individual with the ability to turn into an anthropomorphic canine in conjunction with the lunar cycle. Even with the many cultures which have folklore about these creatures the description of them is about the same. When in animal form these beings look like a wolf or wolf-like canine with the ability of bipedal locomotion, with black to brown fur and a bushy tail. Though the likelihood of a primate to canine metamorphosis is impossible, there is the possibility that these stories and beliefs originate from a biological, flesh and blood source. This source could be Bipedal Canines, as I have stated before. My hypothesis is that in North America it is possible that canines attained the ability of bipedal locomotion. It is possible that individuals who saw these canines considered them as a supernatural being and created the lore of the werewolf. Also with the real-life psychosis lycanthropy, an individual will believe that they themselves can turn into a wolf. So it appears that stories of werewolves were created from a real life psychological and cryptozoological source.

Windigo

Also spelled wendigo, this is a being from Native American folklore. The wendigo originates from the Algonquin tribe who believed the wendigo was a malevolent spiritual being with the ability to possess humans and make them do unspeakable horrors. When the wendigo possesses an individual, it made them become cannibals and yet never be able to quench their hunger. This forever alters that individual into a new creature, a wendigo. Most stories of the wendigo originate in eastern Canada and the Northeast U.S. There are two primary descriptions for the wendigo. The original is of a gaunt human figure with white or grey skin. The modern most common description is of a bipedal creature with the head of a deer with antlers, about 6 to 9 feet, black to brown fur, and human-like arms and legs. The fear of the wendigo was so great that during the late 1800s, there were wendigo trials, similar to werewolf and witch trials of Europe. In original Native American folklore, the wendigo never looked like this. This is the modern interpretation and has since become what people see when they see the wendigo. This is peculiar due to the fact that this being never existed in Native American mythologies. This might be an example of how a cultural idea can form one's reality. When people describe these deer-like beings it's not because they see a wendigo, it is because they think that's what they think it looks like. The wendigo is most likely just a folkloric fictitious monster that has gained a following thanks to modern folklore.

Winnipogo

This is yet another lake creature seen in Canada. The lake this particular cryptid resides in is Lake Winnipegosis in Manitoba, Canada. Lake Winnipegosis is a large lake with a surface area of 2,075 square miles and depth of about 39 feet. The history of this cryptid originates in 1909 when the first documented sightings of a large unknown animal started to occur in the lake. The description of the Winnipogo is similar to the plethora of other aquatic cryptids seen in Canada; a serpentine creature from 10 to 50 feet long with smooth dark colored skin and humps on its back. The name Winnipogo is another play on the name of another lake monster seen in Canada, Ogopogo of lake Okanagen. Due to this lake monster not being as well-known as other Canadian cryptids, there is little research or data for its existence. One prime example for the existence of Winnipogo is an unknown bone discovered in the 1930s, the bone resembles a large vertebrae from an unknown source. Dr James McLeod from the University of Manitoba analyzed the bone and concluded it resembled a vertebra from an extinct cetacean from about 4 million years ago. This has caused some to create the theory that Winnipogo could be an instance of a relic population of extinct cetaceans like the *basilosaurus*. One of the issues for this hypothesis is how a marine mammal found itself in a land locked lake. Another theory states that Winnipogo could be a giant unknown eel like the litany of other lake monsters seen in Canada.

Xing-xing

When most think of unknown primates and China they immediately think of the yeren but there is yet another cryptid primate seen in China. This is the xing-xing, another cryptid primate seen in China. One thing that differentiates the xing-xing to the yeren and the plethora of other cryptid primates seen in Asia is that rather than being humanoid the xing-xing is believed to be more anthropoid. The xing-xing is seen primarily in southern China including the Himalayas and parts of northern Nepal. The xing-xing has a rich anthropological history in China where they see it as similar to both the yeren and yeti. Most stories state that the xing-xing is a peaceful arboreal primate, which if cornered or provoked by humans will attack them. The usual description of the xing-xing is of an ape with long black to red fur, pointed ears, human-like face, and the ability to move bipedally when on the ground for a short period of time. In modern times there still have been sightings of the xing-xing in remote regions of China and northern parts of the Himalayas. Some researchers into the xing-xing believe that it could be another bigfoot-like primate that is seen in Asia. Others think the xing-xing is a relic population of orangutans that once inhabited the Asian mainland. The orangutan hypothesis is most likely, as orangutans are tree dwelling primates and once they are on the ground they've been seen walking on two legs.

Yahoo

The name yahoo is actually a name for several different cryptids of similar descriptions. One of the first uses of the name yahoo is the 1926 novel *Gulliver's Travels* by Jonathan Swift, where those beings were describes as human-like, but brutish and covered in long coarse fur. This description is similar to bigfoot and other cryptid bipeds. In several regions in the U.S and the world the name yahoo is used for a bigfoot-like creature. One of the most well-known instances of this is in Australia where the work yahoo is sometimes used instead of yowie. The name yahoo is yet another colloquial name for sasquatch and other unknown primates. The use for the word yahoo might not just be due to the *Gulliver's Travels*. Yahoo might also be used thanks to the vocalizations of these cryptids. The name yahoo being used for different cryptids across the globe helps demonstrate just how similar these cryptid bipeds are. One great misconception is that all these creatures are the same species, but that is unlikely. Even though cryptids like the yeti, yowie, and almas are described like the North American sasquatch, it doesn't mean they are all the same animal. These creatures are most likely different species and help show how vibrant and diversified the world of cryptozoology is. There are species yet to be discovered and hopefully cryptozoology can help discover these spectacular species.

Yellow Top

Also called Old Yellow Top, this name is for one cryptid seen in the town of Cobalt in Ontario Canada. Sightings of this creature started in 1906. This creature was believed to be a sasquatch, with one distinguishing characteristic; light-colored patches of hair on its head and neck, hence the name Yellow Top. The description of Yellow Top is of a bipedal creature about 6 to 7 feet tall, with a small neck, and short black fur except for a blonde colored mane around the neck and head. The sightings of Yellow Top occurred for about 60 years with the locals around Cobalt seeing a peculiar creature in their local forests. The sightings of Yellow Top abruptly stopped in the 1970s with one of the last sightings being one of the most well-known. It occurred in August of 1970, when several local miners were driving on a deserted road at night when a tall creature crossed the road, almost causing the driver to career into a ditch. To the abrupt stop in sightings caused some to think the Yellow Top had died around that point. With sightings lasting for a period of around 60 years, this might demonstrate how long the average sasquatch lifespan is. The great apes' lifespan varies from 30 to 50 years while humans are around 80 to 100 years. If the lifespan of Yellow Top was presumed to be around 70 to 80 years, this is right between the lifespan of a great ape and a human which would be expected. Most think that the Yellow Top is an example for a marked hominid or just sasquatch with a genetic mutation.

Yeren

The yeren is a cryptid primate seen in the rural provinces of China. The yeren is very similar to the other cryptid primates seen in Asia. The legend of the yeren is an old one, with one of the first recorded mentions of the yeren originating from 206 B.C. Chinese historians recorded the yeren as a "wildman" (the exact translation of the word) living in the forests of their land. The description of the yeren is of a bipedal primate about 5 to 8 feet tall, with red to silver fur, a human-like face and human-like feet. The yeren is believed to be a peaceful creature; when encountered by a human, it would rather run away than create a confrontation. One of the most well-known expeditions to find the yeren occurred in the 1970s, when Professor Zhou Guoxing, one of the most prolific yeren researchers, lead a large team authorized by the Chinese government to hunt for the yeren. In this search the team discovered footprints that weren't from any known animals but still couldn't find conclusive evidence in their search. There are a plethora of theories of what the yeren is; one of the most popular is that the yeren is a relic population of *gigantopithecus*, which did live in China during the late Pleistocene era and is believed to reach heights of up to 9 feet tall. It is possible that *Gigantopithecus* was able to adapt to the changing environment of the Pleistocene and maybe even became smaller in order to hide from the most dangerous predator of all – man.

Yeti

Also known as the abominable snowman, this could be one of the most well-known cryptids in history. The yeti originates from the Himalayan Mountains of Nepal, Bhutan, Tibet, and China. The yeti has been seen around the Himalayas by the indigenous Sherpa people for centuries but the western interest in the creature didn't really start in the 1920s. This is when Europeans started to go to the Himalayas to conquer its magnificent mountains and while there discovered the legend of the yeti. The description of the yeti is either a large bipedal primate about 5 to 9 feet tall, with red to black fur, or a large bear-like creature that kills yaks and people. One of the first westerners to hear of the yeti was Lieutenant-Colonel Charles Howard-Bury in 1921. The most well-known instance of yeti evidence occurred in 1951 discovered by Eric Shipton, who found a line of large footprints in the Himalayas. Another instance of physical evidence for the yeti were the Pangboche hand and yeti scalp. The Pangboche hand was taken out of the Himalayas and later lost, but most believe most likely it originated from a human. The other piece of evidence, the yeti scalp, was later found out to be from an ungulate not a primate. The common belief is that the yeti could be another unknown primate like sasquatch. Later DNA testing discovered that the yeti is an ancient species of polar bear. This might prove that the yeti is not a primate but an unknown species of bear.

Yowie

The yowie is a large cryptid primate seen in Australia. The story of the yowie begins in the oral tradition of the indigenous Aborigines which state that the yowie is a large human-like creature that could be violent if needed. The description of the yowie is of a humanoid primate about 5 to 8 feet tall, with long black to red fur, a bulky powerful body, and humanoid 5-toed footprints. Later when Europeans came to Australia, they began encountering the yowie. The settlers thought that the yowie was responsible for killing their livestock like sheep and goats. One of the first references towards the yowie was in 1795, when a person supposedly saw a yowie on their farm. Even today there have been several sightings of the yowie. One region that has most of the sightings is New South Wales, especially in the Blue Mountain range. One thing that is always brought up with the yowie is the question of how did a large ape get to Australia? Australia doesn't have any indigenous primates. One idea is that possibly extinct hominids and apes from Asia were able to get to Australia. Most yes no to this due to the Wallace Line which separates Asian and Australian animals, but evidence against this is homo floresiensis which is believed to originate from populations of Homo-erectus that came from Asia. It is possible these hominid species via land bridges and rafts were able to get to Australia. Once they reached Australia they became larger in order to survive alongside the other megafauna found in Australia at the time.

Zuiyo-Maru Monster

The story of the Zuiyo-Maru monster starts April 25, 1977, off the coast of New Zealand. The Japanese fishing boat *Zuiyo-Maru* caught a perplexing carcass in their trawl. The crew thought that the creature that they caught was a new unknown species of aquatic creature, possibly a *plesiosaur* or sea serpent. Before the captain of the ship, Akira Tanaka, decided to dump the carcass back into the sea the crew took measurements, photographs, sketches of the body and even tissue samples from the creature. The body was about 30 feet long with a 3 to 5 foot, a long neck, four flippers, a 6-foot-long tail, the tissue was red in color, and weighed about 2 tons. The common theory of what the creature was is that it was an extinct *plesiosaur* that had died and then caught by the *Zuiyo-Maru*. This was so believed that even two Japanese professors, Tokio Shikama and Dr. Fujiro Yasuda thought that this globster was a relic *plesiosaur*. With this later analysis of the creature scientists conclude that the carcass was not an unknown animal but a basking shark. This is just another prime example of jumping to conclusions due the peculiarity of a creature. This example also demonstrates just how important it is to truly analyze evidence due to the fact that there are still mysterious creatures out there but several times these animals are confused with known species. Even though this creature was revealed to be a known species it still shows how there are mysteries out there and that one should never stop exploring.